Home Front Girl

Home Front Girl

A DIARY OF LOVE, LITERATURE,
AND GROWING UP
IN WARTIME AMERICA

JOAN WEHLEN MORRISON

EDITED BY SUSAN SIGNE MORRISON

CHICAGO
REVIEW
PRESS

Published by Chicago Review Press, Incorporated
814 North Franklin Street
Chicago, Illinois 60610

ISBN 978-1-61374-457-4

Interior design: PerfecType, Nashville, TN
All interior images from the author's collection.

Library of Congress Cataloging-in-Publication Data
Morrison, Joan.
   Home front girl : a diary of love, literature, and growing up in wartime
America / Joan Wehlen Morrison ; edited by Susan Signe Morrison. — 1st ed.
      p. cm.
   Includes index.
   ISBN 978-1-61374-457-4
   1. Morrison, Joan—Diaries. 2. Morrison, Joan—Childhood and youth.
3. Schoolgirls—Illinois—Chicago—Diaries. 4. Chicago (Ill.)—Social life
and customs—20th century. 5. World War, 1939–1945—United States.
6. Chicago (Ill.)—Biography. I. Morrison, Susan Signe, 1959– II. Title.

F548.54.M67A3 2012
977.3'042092—dc23
[B]

                                        2012027068

Printed in the United States of America
5 4 3 2 1

To my mother, Joan, whose cheer,
humor, wisdom, and loving presence abide.
I miss you.

Saturday, December 28, 1940

The world's not going to come back the way it was. . . .
London is brave somehow—burning and huddled in
shelters, yet walking also in the unlighted streets. . . .
London is Troy. Everyone is wrong, nobody is right:
Berlin is Troy too. . . . Paris is fallen. Where is Helen? . . .
Oh, world!

Contents

Preface

More than 70 years ago, the United States entered World War II after the bombing of Pearl Harbor on December 7, 1941. In this book, one voice allows us to eavesdrop on what everyday Americans thought and felt about that conflict.

After my mother, Joan Wehlen Morrison, died in 2010, my two older brothers and I found hundreds of poems and journal entries she had composed, starting from when she was nine years old in 1932. Not seen in seven decades, this time capsule allows us to witness the life of a young American girl growing up in Chicago in the wake of the Depression, with World War II nearing and, later, beginning.

Readers have an abiding interest in normal people's lives during extraordinary times. The great popularity of historical fiction, period films, and even lines of dolls that embody different eras attests to this fact. The published diary of a *real* American girl living in the late 1930s and early 1940s, however, is unique. As most of the participants who experienced World War II are aged or dead, discovering a fresh voice from that period adds a new dynamic to a time that has long been closed to us.

Home Front Girl contains a large selection of Joan's journal entries, which are identified by date—the years 1937 to

1943—and ordered chronologically as she ages from 14 to 20. Some journals are missing, including her first one and another from September 1939 through November 1940. The ones we found contain much more than what you see here. How did I choose which sections to transcribe and make public? One of my goals in editing was to include passages I felt were of historical interest, but I also picked those that retained Joan's humor and philosophical outlook. And, given Joan's poetic temperament, I kept some that were, quite simply, stylistically beautiful.

Spelling errors have been corrected (though some preferred spellings of the era, such as "faery" rather than "fairy," are left intact). Minor style inconsistencies have been standardized for ease of reading, and some words or lines within individual entries have been cut in the service of concision. Joan also used a lot of ellipses; I have retained them when she used them to indicate emotional reflection or the passage of time but deleted them if they proved distracting. Otherwise, the text has been left exactly as Joan wrote it. The illustrations that decorate these pages are Joan's own.

In addition to uncovering her diaries, we found a great deal of poetry that parallels her personal love life and the war, as well as short stories that were written both during and after the war years. A small selection of these writings are included here, but more can be accessed at www.homefront girldiary.com.

This volume contains the reflections of a teenage girl living in a historically fraught time. The only daughter of a working-class Swedish immigrant with socialist political convictions and his wife, Joan was born in Hinsdale, Illinois, on December 20, 1922, but grew up in Chicago. Like many girls of working-class families, she found employment herself, most regularly as a camp counselor every summer. She also volunteered at various organizations, such as Billings Hospital and the House of Happiness, where she taught nature study to children. As a scholarship student at the University of Chicago "junior college" (junior and senior years in high school) and then as an undergraduate at the U of C from 1940 to 1944, Joan was an intelligent, humorous, insightful, self-mocking, and pensive reader of her times and the people around her. Her diary gives us an impression of certain aspects of cultural and psychological importance not readily seen in history books. Joan weaves personal reflections on love, nature, and God with commentary on contemporary political events.

Habitually late for school, Joan shows her naïveté throughout her diary. For example, she indicates sympathy for Charles Lindbergh's isolationism before the entry of the United States into the war. She interweaves the hijinks of her high school and college crowd with insights into cultural events. She hears radio shows (no television then!) and goes to the movies quite often (no streaming films on her computer). Her love life is that of a typical teenager—she realizes when she is experiencing a "silly" crush and relates how various passions peter out or develop into "necking."

Joan offers us more than mere historical color. She alternates between being a flighty teenager and a budding poet; she falls passionately—and frequently—in love; she makes fun of herself yet reflects seriously on political crises, nature, religion, and poetry. Her reactions to world events can be profound reflections on the impending death of her generation. As early as 1937, Joan believes that the year 1940 will be a decisive year in history. A pacifist, she learns to bandage for the Red Cross and works in a factory inspecting cans for the war. Joan's passion for classical literature and culture enables her to see the bombings of London and Berlin as examples of another Troy, the city tragically besieged by the ancient Greeks in Homer's epic, *The Iliad.*

Her school notebooks, which she kept while she was an undergraduate at the University of Chicago from 1940 to 1944, likewise contain information about a young adult's life in the early 1940s. Found tucked in between the covers were two pamphlets, one on "Wartime Canning of Fruits, Vegetables." The other, from the Association of American Railroads in Washington, DC, warns, "Don't Waste Transportation": "[A] large part [of the Pullman sleeping cars and passenger coaches] are assigned to troop service—and the armed forces have first call on all the rest. . . . Plan ahead—avoid weekends and holidays—travel light." Joan copied over detailed instructions on how to knit "Men's Heavy Gloves," as knitting was one way that girls could support the war effort.

Not all the information in her notebooks is utilitarian. In psychology class on January 19, 1943, after notes about Pavlov's dogs and conditioned responses, Joan wrote, "Dog gets neurotic if compelled to make too fine a distinction. Me too." Then she drew a picture of a dog salivating. Amongst her scribbles about John Donne's poetry, igneous rocks, and Aztec gods are doodles of girls' heads and dresses, the actress Dorothy Lamour, and an "anthropologist gone native" in his sarong. She also played hangman and calculated her menstrual period. In May 1943 she even jotted down, below her English poetry homework, a list of 34 boys she dated, starting from when she was in elementary school. (Joan wrote this list shortly before her wedding to my father, Robert "Bob"

Thornton Morrison. He is noted near the bottom.) There are numerous messages to her friend Betty Crawford. These entries vary from the frivolous ("Look at the long haired lad in the row ahead" and "Oh, this is deadly," evidently concerning a boring lecture in history class) to the conversational ("Are you going to Northwestern next quarter?") to the epic ("Germany Declared War This Morning!!!").

As an anthropology major at the University of Chicago, Joan was told, quite seriously, by one of her male professors that the only way a woman could become an anthropologist was to marry one. Joan would have seen these journals with the eye of an anthropologist. She believed that everyone has a story, even though he or she may not yet realize what it is. As she presciently wrote on October 19, 1941, "To understand one's story is to weep with pity." In her school notebooks for her History 201 class, Joan jotted down information from Allan Nevins's *The Gateway to History* (1938) and reminds herself to read some chapters in Edward Gibbon's *The History of the Decline and Fall of the Roman Empire.* Then she wrote, "The true historian puts into history his imagination and the projection of his own soul into the facts." Interestingly, Nevins became the so-called father of oral history, the kind of historian Joan became later in life. In a way, this book is her own oral history, unearthed from file cabinets not accessed for decades. She pours her soul into the events that transpire on the world stage.

Robert Maynard Hutchins, the president of the University of Chicago at the time, was an idol for Joan, as her journal makes clear. When she heard his speech, "The Proposition Is Peace: The Path to War Is a False Path to Freedom," on the radio in March 1941, she enthusiastically embraced its sentiments. In her journal, she seems naive enough at this point to mistake the isolation endorsed by the America First Committee as simply a philosophy of peace. Nevertheless, the seeds of her later activism against war had been sown.

Many years later, in addition to supporting presidential candidates against the Vietnam War, she wrote an op-ed column that appeared in the *New York Times* on May 1, 1975. The headline read "Pax," which is Latin for "peace." In the article, Joan reflected on the ending of the war between Vietnam and the United States and the death of her nephew in Vietnam. She pleaded for the country to reconcile after the national trauma: "What has happened has been a sorrow for all of us. Let us mourn our loss but not divide ourselves over the open grave. I'll agree not to say we never should have gone into Vietnam if you'll agree not to say we should have given them more. Okay? Pax."

By this time, Joan had been married for more than 30 years to Bob Morrison, a graduate student in chemistry at the U of C. They met on Washington's birthday—Sunday, February 22, 1942—and were married on June 19, 1943. (They were married for almost 67 years; Bob died two months after Joan did.) After graduating from the University of Chicago in 1944, she and Bob traveled to many US cities while he was in the Navy. Bob became an ensign and a radar instructor. Later, he was assigned to a destroyer captained by the famous PT boat leader John Bulkeley. The war ended before Bob had to be sent to the Pacific. Bob and Joan moved to New York City, where he became a professor of organic chemistry and eventually a famous writer in his own right, as coauthor of *Organic Chemistry*, the standard textbook for a number of decades. Joan, meanwhile, wrote for women's magazines such as *Glamour* and *Mademoiselle* in the late 1940s and early 1950s. After the birth of their children—Bobby, Jimmy, and Susie (me)—the family moved to Morristown, New Jersey.

Joan became a freelance writer for the *New York Times* and later was the coauthor of *American Mosaic: The Immigrant Experience in the Words of Those Who Lived It* (1980), which was recognized as a *New York Times* Notable Book of the Year. Her second book, *From Camelot to Kent State: The Sixties Experience in the Words of Those Who Lived It* (1987), cowritten with my brother Bobby, became the basis for her popular course on the 1960s at the New School for Social Research in New York City. Joan took the raw transcripts of interviews with people who had immigrated or were involved in 1960s political events and uncovered the essence of the narrative within. She often compared the work of the oral historian to that of Michelangelo, the famous artist, who commented on how, while sculpting, he just hewed away the stone to reveal the statue within. I hope I've succeeded in doing that with her journal entries.

In all her work, Joan sees certain events as indelibly "marking" individuals—whether it's the process of immigration or the social unrest of the 1960s. World War II "marked" Joan. She came to mean something new. Her journals not only reflect but also reshape her reality—they are a space where other worlds open up. And through our sharing in these moments of potential, we can reshape our relationships to World War II and how we see it. As a historian herself, Joan would have been thrilled to know that young people will read her writings, composed when she was a young adult. Joan would ask you to consider what events "mark" you indelibly in our society at this time. In a way, it's our obligation to figure out what marks our generation and then respond to it, understand it, and write about it.

I have come to believe in the value of writing a journal—on paper, not on an electronic medium like a blog. True, with a handwritten journal you cannot include links to cool websites or pop-ups or have a soundtrack. But nothing can replace the physical presence of the ink trails carefully traced by a human hand. Especially those made by a beloved human hand. I worked through my grief at my mother's death by editing and transcribing her words: reading them, entering her mindset as a young girl and then a teenager, laughing at her jokes, reflecting on her innocence, gaining her wisdom, and aching for her failed romances—tragic love affairs that I knew were, in the long run, hardly tragic.

Even when she was 19, my mother realized the value of the very journal she was writing, though I'm sure she never expected to have her 52-year-old daughter discover in it the consolation I have found. She commented on January 20, 1942:

> I believe I have written [my diary] with the intention of having it read someday. As a help, not only to the understanding of my time—but to the understanding of the individual—not as me—but as character development. Things we forget when we grow older are written here to remind us. A help not only in history, but in psychology. . . . If I can do that, I believe I shall have done all that I could wish to. I rather like the idea of a social archeologist pawing over my relics.

Well, I'm no social archeologist—I'm just a daughter—but, in my journey toward healing after her loss, I have found comfort so profoundly from the material presence of her notebooks. My mother touched the very two-ring binders whose lined sheets I turn carefully so that the paper won't crumble. She sketched little drawings of herself in outfits and hairstyles now charmingly dated. Only through the tangibility of her composition, inscribed in blue ink that is sometimes blotched or faded, does the human being who composed them come alive. These are precious talismans to me. The young, vital, pensive, perceptive, and creative woman lives not just in my memory but through these pages. With them, I am able to revive the complex, beloved woman I knew—and know—as my mother.

The writings you compose may be touched one day by your children, your grandchildren, or readers of another generation. The very act of making contact with what you personally touched will be so meaningful to them. Your insights to your time will make the past blaze up into life for them, and with that kindled light, your essence will glow as well.

—Susan Signe Morrison

Home Front Girl

d never get there. Tuesday Be
Wednesday, Purr, Thursday
Icecabbe. I swore no one
was to stop me today. Just
[S]loria came along & we both
must diet loungling. Poor
loria. But she departed
at over there without her &
[j]ust as I was slipping into
Phy Sci I heard her little
voice "John". But I was dete-
ined & dragged her back with
me... and her friend too,
some girl who had a com-
plete already. Then Bill c-
 and sat down next
me. Stevenson was very
okay — Funny and self
he poured carbon diox-
(you couldn't see it) into
a paper bag & it went c-
It was spooky. Other e-
ith glasses too. Oh (He's so
[re]ligious. Yesterday he le[ft]
Bunson Burner go[ing]

1937

Age 14

"I felt like Hilter or Mussolini or Stalin or somebody."

Tuesday, April 13, 1937

Hello! Tests next week! Oh boy! Have pity on me and sympathize.

Today I rang the bell after first lunch. Oh, but it was beautiful. Yesterday, you see, Sheldon promised me that I could ring it, so today I appeared and did so. I just pushed it and everyone started rushing around. I felt like Hitler or Mussolini or Stalin or somebody—(not Eddie VIII*).

Monday, April 19, 1937

Mr. Lucas thinks I'm a communist. Today in Study, you see, Ruth and I were—well—you know—doing Latin together.

---

*He became Duke of Windsor after abdicating the throne in December 1936 to marry Wallis Simpson, an American divorcée.

Which isn't approved of. Then Alice asked me what *onomato-poeia* is and, while I was explaining, Mr. L. came over and said, "Can't you work by yourself?" to me. "Are you helping these girls or are they helping you?" And I said, "Well, it's sort of community work, you see." And he said, "Well, you know we can't have a lot of little communities in study hall." And I said, thinking of Latin, "No, but why not one big commu-nity." I guess he must have thought I was a communist then, 'cause he looked sort of frightened and said we'd better work alone. And I said, "Uh-huh." And that was that. Once before he made me (and Ruth) stand in the corner for community work—me the socialist! And I had my red sweater on, too!

Tuesday, April 20, 1937

Hello! Do you realize it's spring! Spring. And the weather's lovely (only it rained) and the air is sweet (sometimes) and the grass is green (in patches) and there isn't a handsome boy in [Horace] Greeley [Elementary School]! It's positively outra-geous! And on top of *that*, there isn't any R.O.T.C.* unit in Greeley (they do look so handsome in uniforms!). When we went to the main building for the music festival, they were there in their uniforms and looked so gorgeous! And to top *that*, they're even discussing doing away with the R.O.T.C. on account of putting war into [the] open minds (?) of the boys! Phooey, what about the uniforms, we don't think about war. (Or do we?) Which all goes to show that spring is wrong . . .

Thursday, April 29, 1937

On the way back to the baseball field, we passed two boys who made two remarks on seeing Betty and me—remark the first:

*Reserve Officers' Training Corps.

"Look—the mosquitoes are out already"—meanwhile looking directly at us. Also, there were no real mosquitoes out. Mmm? Remark the second: "Hi ya, good-looking." Now, of course, no person in his right senses would address either Betty or me as "good-looking," but these boys didn't look very sensible. Anyhow, what we're trying to find out was which remark—(if either)—was referring to us. Mom says they probably meant we were good-looking mosquitoes, but I wonder, now . . .

Sunday, May 2, 1937

I went downtown yesterday to Art Institute and saw the Mayday communist parade—very scraggly and the uniforms looked like they'd been thro' the war—the Civil War.

P.S. In church, I was indirectly referred to as a "little girl" four times and directly twice! "Little girl" indeed! I'm 14½ yrs. old and 5 ft. 1½ inches high! "Little girl"—humph!

Monday, May 3, 1937

Got my hair set today. In my opinion, if I had hollower cheeks, I'd be a perfect double for Garbo.*

Thursday, May 6, 1937

Hello! The German zeppelin *Von Hindenburg* crashed not three hours ago at Lakehurst, New Jersey. That great new sister ship to the *Graf Zeppelin*!! Just burnt up like that. The radio announcer said it was 'cause the lightening set fire to the explosive hydrogen in the ship and then it exploded. Airships seem to have a curse or something—to everyone except the *Graf* Something disaster has happened. Now the *Graf* is

*Greta Garbo was a famous actress. She was originally from Sweden but became a huge hit in Hollywood.

the only one left. The *Herald Examiner* said 100 people were killed, but as it's a Hearst paper, 50 is a safer guess. They always exaggerate!* Ho-hum—must read about Renaissance art now—um—um.

Good Night!

Wednesday, May 12, 1937

This day is the 12th of May in the year 1937 and it was Coronation Day. I woke up at five o'clock, turned off the alarm, awoke again at six and listened to the actual coronation. I bundled up in all my blankets, leaving one ear out, and sat on the sofa listening.

I heard George pronounced and anointed King and Elizabeth Queen.† Wonder what Edward VIII who abdicated is thinking tonight. When they sang "God Save the King," while I was putting on my stocking, I simply listened like a loyal Englishwoman. I would have even stood up, except for the cold and I couldn't stand on one foot. I just sort of listened and thought of the peoples of all colors in all lands who were

---

*William Randolph Hearst was a newspaper magnate whose papers were reputed to be sensationalizing.
†These are the parents of Queen Elizabeth II.

6

listening and wondered what they thought. (That shows what reading Kipling* can do—it's made me a better Englishman than American.) Well, Coronation or no Coronation—there was school today.

The whole school practically—maybe 400—went to see *Romeo and Juliet* at [a] special 10¢ rate. *Romeo and Juliet* was really beautiful. Especially Norma Shearer who played the part of Juliet. She's so classic—really. Classic. Betty and I went together and of course got into a mess. She didn't have her note from home so she wrote herself one and signed a teacher's name. The teacher had given Betty permission to come. Well, it so happened that same teacher who was taking tickets was the same one whose name Betty signed. So Betty said sweetly, "I gave myself permission to come and signed your name." I don't believe the teacher has recovered yet, but Betty got in. O, shades of Shakespeare had he been there (at the show) to hear all Greeley titter every time Romeo kissed Juliet—shades of Shakespeare! Good Night!

Friday, May 21, 1937

Oh, I went down and saw them today at Soldier's [sic] Field. Who? Why the R.O.T.C. boys in the annual review. Eight thousands troops there were—8,000—and probably 50,000 young folk in the audience. Mayor Kelly was there and oh—biggest news of all!—Lake View—Lake View—the school I'll attend next year—won the first place along with St. Mel High School!! Isn't that marvelous! About Lake View, I mean! My own school!

---

*Rudyard Kipling, English poet who often described the colonies of the British Empire. He won the Nobel Prize in Literature and is famous for books such as *The Jungle Book*.

"Breathes there a girl with soul so dead,
Who never to herself has said,
'This is my own, my darling school.' "*
Anyhow, Lake View won.

The review was at Soldier's [*sic*] Field—a beautiful place, you know, open air—near the Lake—classical pillars on either side. It might have been a Roman forum or something.

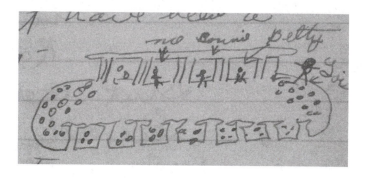

If there only had been some gladiators to be eaten by lions, it would have been a perfect Roman arena.

The sky was pretty threatening for a while and it even rained a few drops, but for the Grand Finale with all 8,000 troops in uniform the sun came up in glory to behold the sight of it. They all looked so tall and young and proud. It must be the pagan in me but when I saw all those boys so much like soldiers in their khaki uniforms and guns—and swords and solemn, eager faces—why, my heart just thrilled for the pure glory of them in the breaking sunlight. They all looked so bright and strong and fair and brave besides—well, I might have been Caesar himself so gladsome was I at the sight.

---

*Parody of Sir Walter Scott's poem "The Lay of the Last Minstrel."

And then Lake View was presented with her prized colors and the band burst into "The Star-Spangled Banner" and we stood up and shouted for our anthem, glad, and school.

"A hundred thousand voices.

Raised in proud salute."

Isn't that pretty—of course there were only 50,000, but what's the difference? It's pretty just the same. . . .

Saturday, May 29, 1937

I have walked downtown and back today—about eight miles I guess and, oh, it's so lovely out. Glorious you know—full flush of spring—tulips at their brightest—blossoming reds and purples startingly vivid on the green. Sky as blue as ever could be and lake as blue-green—as—as—as—as, well, as the lake. Lilac bushes shedding loveliness and the pool in the park just covered with floating fallen petals. Bright-haired children reaching up to sniff vivid flowers or racing around 'plashing fonts in the park. (Excuse me if I get poetical—I walked eight miles).

Then going on to the Art Institute—lovely pictures—and pretty little garden in the center—the one I like. Sort of a relief to see cool white marble and green grass after all the color—but I do love the color. Then out to see the splendid "Fountain of the Great Lakes." Lovely Goddess of the Waters pouring from her shell onto the sister lakes with nymphs sporting on the side. Then to the library—Kipling—then walked home along [the] lovely lake with elongated purple shadows thrown along the sands. Still bright-haired children playing—still flowers no less vivid or sky less blue—sun like blood in the West. Oh I felt the glory and the spring of Kipling's poem—

But as the faithful years return
And hearts undaunted sing again.*

Isn't that a lovely thought—"hearts undaunted sing again"—though ever the years are long and hard—the Spring will always come and our hearts can sing again—oh how beautiful!!!

Ever and again today I wondered at the infinite magnitude of God to give so unsparingly of beauty—what artist ever splashed his colors so boldly or to better effect than He? The dandelion may be a weed, but when I saw it glowing in lusty color, I thought it the loveliest, brightest, most glorious day-flower in the whole wide world. There's something about Spring which makes you feel good and pure and free and—trusting—and more religious than ever a church could—because the world is the only real church and Spring is the bedecked altar. And surely it is not wrong to worship the Spring because God is all that is Good and Beautiful as is the spring. Oh that's how I feel now.

I feel so glorious and uplifted and my heart is just bursting with spring and love of the world and life.

Well—maybe my feet will hurt in the morning but I certainly feel grand now—

Good Night.

P.S. Thank Heaven for Kipling!

Sunday, May 30, 1937

This is Memorial Day and it rained. Daddy and I went out for a walk and when it rained went under a tree near the

---

*From Kipling's "Merrow Down"; Joan changes "unwounded" to "undaunted."

statue of the Unknown Soldier. He looked so lonely there in the rain (the Soldier, I mean), and there wasn't even a wreath to mark the day. It seemed so pitiful. So I picked a little flower from the tree and ran in the rain to lay it at his feet. And I'm sure he knew I did it and was glad that some-one remembered him on this day. It was only a little flower, but I'm sure it meant as much as a wreath. I'm glad I did it, as I'm sure the Soldier is.

Thursday, October 7, 1937

Hello! Here I am again, after all these years—or at least three months. You know I've been at camp for two of those months and—oh so much happened!* And now school's started and I'm a sophomore!!! I taught nature study all summer at camp—three classes a day and the flower table to take care of, which makes me feel quite responsible—and they called me "*Miss* Joan." I think that was the crowning glory of my life— "Miss Joan"—and all my pupils called me that. . . .

There were dances every Saturday night, of course, and I had a great deal of fun at them. *He* came out once every two weeks over the weekend so I did see *him* and even spoke with *him*. The very last night at the very last dance *he* asked me for the very last waltz and oh—gosh! And the last morning, just before the train left, *he* made me the acorn ring *he* had prom-ised. But—well, anyhow, I—like him. There was another nice boy out there—Andy was his name. He's quite good-looking and I liked him too. He also taught nature study and we often discussed birds. He had made a list of all the birds he saw

---

*Joan was a counselor at two camps. In 1937 and 1938 she worked at Arden Shore Camp in Lake Bluff, Illinois, a camp for poor children and those at risk for delinquency.

that summer and it was terribly long—I should have made one too.

I was more alive this summer I think than I had ever been before. I mean really *alive*—not just breathing and eating. I used to go to bed at night all full of something or other—either terribly happy or terribly glad—always so full of things that it hurt. During the last two weeks for awhile I thought I would burst—I expected to be so unhappy that it was almost a relief to look forward to it and say, "Monday will be the awfullest day." You see Monday was the nature pageant—I did not expect to get anything there and, after lights out, there was the honor service, and I certainly didn't expect an honor bracelet! Well, Saturday was the worst day in the summer for me—I went to bed so full of pent-up unhappiness I could hardly sleep.

Then Sunday things began to change—I mean the relief of expecting the awfulness [of] Monday almost comforted me. Then Kathryn and I were invited to the Scott Honor Service and went over to [the] Brownie [cabin] to pass the evening. All the other Peppers* were on a hike. Andy and *he* were there, and we four talked and played records and discussed music, the zodiac and the baseball teams until it got dark enough for the Scott Service. Then Kathryn and I went to that.

It was down by the lake—with the waves grey and angry and the moon dull red as it had been the night I got my Scott Honor pin. We sat there and the Honor girl lit the fire as I had long ago and said the words that I had said and took the oath that I had taken and thought the thoughts that I had thought—not so long ago. It made me feel the way I had when I got my pin—happy and sad—and wanting to burst.

---

*A group of campers.

Then the Scotts went up the hill and Kathryn and I went up last of all. When we reached the head of the stairs we walked over to the bluff and stood in front of the log facing the lake and the moon. Just as we stood there alone, dark taps began to play—timed so perfectly that it seemed for the moment that we were in a magic circle of moonlight and music. Then the enchantment ceased and we went back along the white shadowy road through the sleeping camp to our cottage and got into bed. All the unhappiness I had felt the night before was fled and I slept as I had the night I got the Scott pin a year ago. The next day was tense because of the night that was to follow, but as evening came on I again felt the relief that I *knew* I was to be disappointed.

Then the pageant began and indeed it was lovely—the king and queen of nature dressed in Grecian gowns on the Sacred Carpet and all the procession of children following them. Really the pageant was lovely. Then the award-giving time came—and oh—I got my tree badge and my Star Book!

Then, after the moon was above, the Great Spirit walked around the circle and picked out Beverly Kennelly and me, Joan Wehlen, as honor bracelet girls. Oh—and we repeated the pledge with unbelief in our hearts and surprise in our eyes—"I promise to live up to the meanings of the lighted candles—to never let their light grow dim through lack of courage or because of difficulties." And Beverly and I could not—we did not—cry as some girls do, but just stood and looked at each other and the bracelets—I wear [mine] this minute.

And all that night I lay with the Star Book and tree badge beneath my pillow and held my wrist in the moonlight to see the bracelet shine. I really thought I was dreaming all through that evening.

The next morning we got up early and went swimming *in naturalibus* and it really is a grand thing to swim unhampered out of a grey sea into the sunrise. I had never seen the sun rise before, and he slid rather grandly from the grey. Then we went up cold and shivering as we gazed upon our bracelets. That night was the last dance and *he* asked me for the last waltz and we danced it together and went back to Pepperville—he and I and some others. Then everyone played Farmer in the Dell, Streets and Alleys* and London Bridge and Red Rover and I went to bed terribly happy.

The next morning I asked him for the acorn ring he had promised me, but he said he hadn't finished it yet. So we went back to the kitchen and he borrowed a knife and made it right there before the trains left.

And that night I slept at home.

So now I'm in high school and a sophomore and have been called "Miss Joan" and taught nature study and am in the honor society so you must treat me with proper respect, dear diary.

Good Night.

Monday, November 15, 1937

Lake View [High School] had an Open House Friday night and Mrs. Turner, my ex–English teacher, told Mother I'd be a great writer someday—Hm . . . hm . . .

---

*A chase game.

I got a nice piece in the *Lake reView**** about me—see.[†] You see, I take care of the "Vox Pop"[‡] column and it got the Greeley headline and took up most of the Greeley column besides, so I feel pretty good. Besides that, I contributed enough news to add to the rest of the column besides. I feel so elated!

Sunday, November 21, 1937

When I asked Mrs. Topping who'd be famous from our school for the paper and how, she said me—in journalism. That's two teachers said that in one week. I'm getting hopeful. . . .

Monday, November 22, 1937

We're writing expository compositions in English—heaven help us! Some of the subjects are quite humorous and edifying—

"How to Taste Your Sister's First Fudge"

"How to Get More Peanuts for Your Penny"

"How to Avoid Promptness" (that's mine)

"How to Sleep in Study Hall" (ditto)

"How to Pass a Hall Guard Without a Pass" (we tried that last and it worked—past three hall guards)

Geometry is awful!

Phooey to Euclid—(he invented it)

Phooey to Mrs. Uhlir—(she thinks she teaches it)

Phooey to me—(I don't know it)

Well—Good Night.

---

*The school newspaper is still called the *Lake reView*.

†Joan pasted a clipping here that reads, "Joan Wehlen, from room 201, deserves honorable mention for her fine contributions to our column this week. Thank you, Joan."

‡*Vox populi* means "voice of the people." "Vox Pop" refers to Joan's column in which students are interviewed or quoted.

Tuesday, November 23, 1937

Compositions in English tomorrow. Mrs. T. said they had to be serious so I wrote on "How to recover dead bodies from the water." Surface Diving, you know. That's serious enough—if you're dead!

I'm still trying to think of a middle name—must have it by Saturday. What do you think of—Mary, Ursula, Margaret, Patricia, Louise, or Holly—I just don't think anymore. . . .

Friday, November 26, 1937

Yesterday was Thanksgiving and—leave it to me—I passed out in church. You see, I'm in the choir and it was over-heated up there and the robes were heavy and we had to kneel for ever so long on high prayer cushions and I got hot and couldn't stay up any longer—The girl next to me saw it and whispered that she'd take me out after the "Agnus Dei." When it was over, I started to go out but luckily the fella behind me (the tenor solo) grabbed my arm and practically led me out. Then the girl with me followed and he got me a drink and rushed around after the janitor to get the key. He had a solo to sing then, so he went back and the girl made me lie down and be comfy. I never fainted before. I feel so old-fashioned and idiotic. It's not in style to faint anymore, you see. The faint-at-a-breath maiden is no longer "it," but could I help it?

Sunday, November 28, 1937

Hello! I was confirmed today at St. Peter's. I took Louise for my middle name. It means "pugnacious" so I don't know—I like "Brietta" much better. For some reason the name attracts me; it's so odd, and the meaning is "bright, shining." Isn't that pretty—"Brietta." I got to church early today (surprise to all) but it was too late to change the name anyhow—you see, I just found Brietta yesterday—though I've been looking for it for a long time.

[Later, I] came home and said, "Don't disturb me— I'm going to do Geometry," and proceeded to read a Conan Doyle* book—(not on Geometry). I guess I'll do the Geometry tomorrow—maybe—I hope, I hope. Well, Geometry we have always with us.

Wednesday, December 8, 1937

Last week Mrs. Topping read my "Lonesome Pine" composition to the class and said it was writing at its best. Ah! Then she asked the class if they didn't feel something good in it—so they said "no," but Mrs. T. appreciates me—I hope.

Last Saturday I went downtown and saw Santa Claus, etc. They've got the cutest dolls there—I want one for Xmas even if I am almost 15—but I want a set of O. Henry,† too— even more. Honestly, I'm practically a little girl when it comes to Xmas displays. I'll stand for an hour and watch someone demonstrate "DyDee" dolls or something.

I picked up a book, *German in Easy Lessons*, downtown and had already learned that all nouns begin with capitals and there are four cases and was just going into verbs (I ought to go to Germany) when the salesgirl came along and seemed to think I was going to read the whole book—so I went—*sans* verbs.

---

*Sir Arthur Conan Doyle wrote the Sherlock Holmes mysteries.
†An American short story writer. His most famous story is "The Gift of the Magi."

I finally finished the *Niebelungenlied*. It's the story of Siegfried and Brunhild, etc., in verse. The real reason I read it was because I wanted to have read one book almost no one else I know has read. Last night I was in the living room reading it alone by lamplight when my mind began to wander (the book has that effect). The window was open and I put my hand out into the night and watched the snow drift into it. All I could see was my white hand and the bits of snow in the blackness. For a moment I saw the unreality of everything except my hand and the snow. It gives you a queer feeling when you seem to know that nothing really exists but you and the night. The street lamps are the same way—little dabs of life in the night—clear etchings for a moment of people who come from darkness and go into it. It's almost frightening when you think of it.

Mrs. Topping's been absent for a couple of days and we've got a funny substitute who reads us stories and looks like Hitler. I hope Mrs. T. comes back soon.

I've been invited to join a girls' club that meets on Fridays—I like the kids in it so I think I will.

Tonight we had choir practice and we tried an old 15th-century plainsong—written in *square* notes. The additionals were all in Old English—it gives you a funny feeling. While we were singing the ancient "Sanctus" and had got to the "Glory" part, someone outside (the choir room has windows on the street) began to laugh—oh, the awfullest laugh—at us. It was hardly human in sound and echoed and re-echoed through the dark corridors downstairs. It frightened us—I suppose it was silly—but the laugh was so awful and disillusioned. In the still church singing the aged songs—(we sang one plainsong written in 348 AD, can you believe it?)—our voices sang the same notes that other voices sang 1,500 years ago —before our language was spoken or America thought of. It makes you seem so nonexistent—we're each so important to ourselves, but in 1,500 years, will those same notes be sung in tongues and places now unknown—

> How many ages hence shall this our
> lofty scene be acted over in states
> unborn and accents yet unknown?*

Shakespeare had the right idea.
I'm scared; where will I be in 1,500 years?
And that laugh breaking the timeless songs with mockery. He was laughing at us. Maybe he knew what 1,500 years will bring—and so he laughed.
What with the hand in the snow and the laugh, I feel very queer—
I'd better do Latin to humanize me. . . .
P.S. I've got the nicest pretend game about our court building.† I imagine it a medieval court because it has wrought iron gates and a lantern on either side. And with snow on the ground and the gates and the lantern *and* my imagination, it does have that look!

Thursday, December 9, 1937

Hello! The funny, Hitler-mustached substitute is still with us. He gives us the craziest assignments. He read some radio sketches to us called "the seven stages of parenthood" and we

---

*From Shakespeare's *Julius Caesar*.
†Their apartment building at 821 Cornelia Avenue had a central court in front of it.

had to write the seventh. I hope Mrs. Topping comes back. No one knows quite what's the matter with her.

My opinion of Mr. Nelson has changed—I think he must be a misplaced genius. You know he never talks in class or anything, so we just concluded that he had nothing to say. Today he brought out some frogs from his mysterious cupboard and let the kids dissect a couple. The thing got too painful to all concerned after a while, so Arnold and I wandered over to inspect the aforementioned cupboard. Most of the stuff in jars there didn't mean a thing to us, so we just looked and wondered. Then Mr. N. came over (evidently dissecting didn't attract him, either) and started to talk to us. He explained about the stuff in jars—he had a cow's heart, and a lot of mosses, and a baby pig before it was born, and some jellyfish and deep sea plants. And honestly—the man's interesting when he talks. Much more than frogs. He's intelligent too, I think. He talked about the junk, etc., and, after about 10 minutes talking (surprising in him), smiled a sort of apologetic smile (he smiled!) and said, "That's all I have—not much"—sort of wistfully—I know he's a misplaced genius.

Then he went away and Arnold and I just looked at each other. We hadn't thought vocal expression possible in Mr. N. Then Arnold said, "The more I see of him—the less I understand him." Which is a profound statement and goes ditto for me. Because if he's a genius, why must he wear bow ties and purple suspenders—it's a real mystery. (But I still think he's a genius.)

Wednesday, December 15, 1937

The other day Japan bombed three American ships*—one a gunboat—that were in some Chinese harbor and everyone thought there was going to be a war—there wasn't though, so it's all right—I hope.

Monday, December 20, 1937

I am 15 years old. Fifteen years ago I was not, now I am—15 years from now—who knows? It gives you a queer feeling—your birthday.

P.S. Italy and Germany and Japan have a triple alliance now—whatever that means. And the Japanese had a peace assembly at Tokyo this week and are still killing people in China—nice world, isn't it?

Christmas Day! December 25, 1937

Hello! It's Christmas Day! Isn't that a lovely word—"Christmas"—the very sound of it makes you think of bright snow and blue stars and shining, laughing things—especially the "Christ" part—the sound of the word is like bright snow or sunlight. The sound of "God" makes you feel strange too. Not like "Christ," not bright and shining, but like something glowing deep within you. Words—some of them—seem to come from the very heart of men—some bright and some deep within you. Words are terribly beautiful—sometimes.

We just heard Dickens' *Christmas Carol* on the radio with Lionel Barrymore as Scrooge. "Scrooge" is another word that sounds like what it means. Deep and somewhat held in.

---

*In the margin, Joan wrote "*Panay* bombing." The *Panay* was the US gunboat bombed on December 12, 1937.

I wonder if words sound like that because of the associations they bring up or because it's really in them—not in us.

I'm sitting in the living room now listening to "Silent Night, Holy Night" and looking at our pretty pagan Christmas tree. It comes of course from a Norse pagan custom—but I guess we're all a little pagan at heart. The tree was supposed to be the symbol of the Nordic or Teutonic nature worship and I rather think all the worshippers have a great deal of the nature god in their hearts. Anyhow, green trees and thick grass and bright growing things get me. Our religion has modified many other religions into itself and that's what makes us come to it. We can't get away from what is in us and nature is very close to our hearts, as are the things that have been.

I can't agree with myself on religion. Sometimes I read things that seem to explain it all and then it all seems to be there, but there's something missing, I know, deep down inside of me. I think if we could understand everything there wouldn't be any use of living. Things a little beyond are so much more beautiful. Promise is greater than fulfillment. Sometimes I'm afraid when people start to explain things—everything, it seems. But there's something in me that won't be explained—and that's what scares me. And trees and the lake and the sky and rain and—me. I do get scared when I start to think. Momma says I shouldn't worry about things—but don't you see—I must—it's me and I can't dismiss it because it's too big for me. And then things attract me that I can't explain. We've got a Buddha on our table and he—just—gets me. It's very soothing to look at him—so of course he can't be wrong. I wonder if anything is.

But Christmas and songs make you feel very believing in beautiful things and very sure about right and wrong. But the wondering is still there—I'm not sure about me.

Wednesday, December 29, 1937

I and another girl walked home. I bought a powder puff and we gossiped. She said—honestly she did!—that I was thin—oh am I? Dear journal—that's such a beautiful word—thin. I do hope I am. All the movie stars are—I only weigh 103—that's not so much, is it?

I was thinking—the star that shone on Christmas Eve the first time must have started to shine about 2,000 years before that, before its light ever got to Earth according to astronomy—I hope that isn't so—it isn't, is it—do you think? I mean, I suppose it's just as wonderful either way, but I'm more used to it the other way. You see, I went to the planetarium last week and heard a lecture on the "Architecture of the Heavens." It's all terribly big—to me.

Sometimes I wonder if I'm really laughing at the things I say or if I mean them. I catch myself saying things and find myself grinning at something—inside, I mean. The world's a pretty inefficient place—the way we run it—but I rather like it.

P.S. "Earth" (spelled with a capital E) is a pretty word, isn't it?

Friday, December 31, 1937

I had the awfullest dream last night. I dreamt a war was begun and people were running about with brightened looks in their eyes. I was a boy and I knew I would have to be a soldier. I was afraid to go to war. I kept seeing trenches and mud and horror and pain and things—and killing people—and I was terribly scared inside. But I knew I would have to join the army anyhow because otherwise people would call me coward. I went to enlist and that's all I remember. I figured I might have three months in a training group before I would have to fight. It was a terrible dream and I was so scared. That's all I remember. . . .

I sit here and wait for the last minutes of 1937 to come to an end. [Nineteen thirty-seven] sounds like such a momentous year—like 1492 or 1066 or 1588 or 1776, doesn't it? I'm sure it marks a crisis in our history. But 1940 sounds even greater—well, we must wait.

I've been reading my journal over, my journal of this year—and plenty seems to have happened. A king has been crowned—England's George VI. Edward married Wallis and closed that part of England's history—or did he? The Spanish Civil (?) War continued and the Japanese began and conquered an undeclared war in China. Now the civilization of thousands of years is under the flag of the rising (or setting?) sun of Japan. Add to things that have happened: the *Hindenburg*, last but one of the great airships, burned to cinders in New Jersey.

P.S. Marconi* also died this year.

---

*Winner of the Nobel Prize in Physics, who was also considered the father of the radio.

1938

Age 15

"[Sixteen] sounds like a lovely age."

Tuesday, January 4, 1938

Well—now it is 1938 and we look forward to this year's events. Doesn't that "8" look nice in the date. Last year I wrote the same thing about the "7" in 1937—I wonder if people will always be so idiotically hopeful. Yet my hopes of last year didn't suffer so much—I don't know what I wish to begin with, but I got a lot—I'm a teacher—"he" danced with me— I've got new friends—more interests, am on school and church paper. Found some good books that I hadn't yet read—but O. Henry, I wish you had written more. I've got an improved (I think) philosophy, another name, Louise—(though—Oh, how I wish I had taken Brietta—Louise is no part of me as Brietta would have been and is!). I've made a decision: I'm going to make Brietta part of my name—Joan Louise *Brietta* Wehlen. How's that? Looks like royalty, it's so long. Oh, by the way, in my achievements of the year, I forgot to mention I had read the *Niebelungenlied*—almost two months it took, and I owed 33¢ at the library by the time I had finished, but now I've read one book very few people I know have read—which is something.

We're reading *As You Like It* (you may not but I do) in English and Shakespeare makes the awfullest puns—worse than Jack Benny*—really!

We're doing circle theorems in Geometry and Burton, who sits behind me, hums music from Wagner's operas all through it—it's very bad for my concentration which isn't so strong naturally anyhow.

I wonder if there'll be a war this year—plus what wars we have now—Europe at boiling pitch (100° C or 212° F). I hope not, but it would be interesting—forgive the thought—Earth is interesting enough now.

January 1938

The Sin of Being Patriotic

If a reasonable man were to look at it (which he never does), he would easily see the foolishness of what we call by the brave word "patriotism." What is this "motherland" we honor? Is it the flag? It cannot be the flag. It is a beautiful thing to be sure—waving brightly in the air, but who will die for a piece of cloth?

You say it is only a symbol; then of what is it a symbol? Of the men who founded [a country] and who have lived in it? No, for who will die for dead men? Is it the living leaders? No, it cannot be. For if half the country acclaim a leader (which, incidentally it never does), why, then the other half must hate

---

*Immensely famous comedian on radio, in movies, and later on television.

him. So it is not the leaders, for who will die for a despised man even if he be president?

Is it, then, the people—can it be? This hungry, seeking people of whom we are a part—whom—though we are of them, we are a part—whom—though we are of them, we laugh at? Who knows? Men have died for less—and for more. Can it then be for less—and for more?

Can it then be this last thing, the land? The good black earth with green things that grow and die again—the good black Earth that will cover us all? Is it this that men die for, the symbol at once of life and death? Is this what we die for— our tomb?

Nay—if men die not for any of these things and yet die, do they die for nothing? Are all the souls buried into Earth for naught? Perhaps it is nothing, but I, too, would die for this wrong and beautiful thing that men call "patriotism."

Yet peace is not so great that we would sell our dreams for her—even if they be foolish dreams.

There is no beginning and no end
No age and no youth
Time you cannot comprehend
Everlasting truth.

Wednesday, January 5, 1938

Went to church for choir practice tonite—the moon, yellow and new, hung tilted in the treetops like an empty cradle—it looked so lovely. And it was frosty out and all the stars were blazing and there were white clouds in the sky—and the air seemed really clear.

Query: if you don't like the way a person talks or seems to think, but if they're nice to you and don't make anyone feel bad, should you still be friendly with her?

Thursday, January 6, 1938

We're still reading *As You Like It* in English. One of the lines goes: "Such a *nut* was Rosalind." I never thought old William so modern.

Burton broke my standing record of being late—he came in at third period today. He *says* he went to the opera last night and was up so late that he slept till French (second period) was over—sounds fishy to me. He saw *Lohengrin* and started to explain how they worked the "swan" business—he's very hazy on it, I must say—he's crazy about Wagner—(pronounced "*V*agner").

Sunday, January 9, 1938

Last night we went to [a] show and saw Norman Alley's *Bombing of the* [USS] *Panay*. Pictures before and after and all. I wonder how he knew when he made them that those pictures would be so important. An historical document—the paper says.

Monday, January 10, 1938

I made up the life of Wagner for music today. It was home-work, but I had forgotten so I did it in study. I knew when he was born and died so I made up what happened in between—gee—feel like the recording angel. I wanted to have him born in a log cabin but I didn't know if they had log cabins in Germany. Do they? Then I wanted him to die in poverty (as all geniuses must) but wasn't sure so I just had him die. But I covered two pages anyhow. Am I good!

Monday, January 17, 1938

You know, we're still reading *As You Like It* in school and the other day Mrs. Topping said that Orlando (he is always late in the play—once he excuses himself by saying "I came within an hour of my promise"—sounds like me) and I would have made a fine pair 'cause we were both always late—a dirty crack if you ask me. Then she said if we ever acted out the play that I should play Orlando 'cause I just came late naturally and anyhow I do make up the loveliest excuses, like Orlando.

Thursday, January 20, 1938

Yesterday a boy asked me if I'd go to a dance on Saturday with him. I told him I'd see—I guess I'll go. His name is Jack Latimer. Imagine—my first date.

Saturday, January 22, 1938

I went for a fitting of my nature study uniform. They're awfully cute—green, of course, with brown buttons and pleats and monograph on the belt—"C.D.F." I hope they're done by the Sunday when we get our pledges. Do I look German—I'm certainly not the flaxen-haired, blue-eyed type (though I *do* look like Marlene Dietrich!*), but anyhow Jean's grandmother is about the fifth person to say I look German this month—now do I or do I not? And then of course "Wehlen" does look German with that "hl" even though it is Swedish.

Jack called for me this night to go to the dance and his father drove us. I wore my brown velvet dress. It was a nice

---

*An actress who was born in Germany but became a star in the United States.

dance. I know several of the kids there. Jack had sprained his ankle yesterday, but he could dance anyhow. He is going to join the R.O.T.C. band and collects stamps. One of my partners was trying to teach me to do the college shag. You sort of hop all over your partner's foot with your right foot and then with the left—that was as far as I got anyhow. My poor partner!

Another fellow and I were dancing—it was a foxtrot and I always count under my breath for that—one-two-three-four, one-two-one-two—so of course there wasn't much *verba** on my part. Finally my partner said, "Nice conversation, isn't it?" and I said, "There's always the weather." So we discussed the weather till we came to the conclusion that there wasn't any. Then more silence. I counted one-two-three-four, one-two-one-two. Then I said, "And then there's the *Panay* incident." So he said, "Oh yes, there's always that," but we had not really got started on that before the dance was over—one-two-three-four, one-two-one-two. . . . Jack's father drove us home too.

Sunday, January 23, 1938

On the way home [Virginia and I] took the bus through the park. It was drizzling darkly out and all you could see from the inside of the bus were the street lamps—little circles of wet light. It was so black-dark out and the lighted bus seemed so all in all itself. As though the whole world were in that little space and we were all that really existed. I felt that way at the camp honor services this summer as though there were nothing but everlasting night beyond the circle of light. Well, anyhow, in this bus it seemed as though we were going through

*Latin for "words."

endless space in some rocket ship of the future—we few odd people—shooting through space—and the street lamps were occasional stars—oh, what a feeling!

Do you ever wonder when you're on the streetcar or in an elevator with a few other people what would happen if you few were suddenly to be the only people left on Earth, as though your bus or car were the only thing saved from some gigantic calamity—how you people would remake systems— if it could be an ideal universe—if the world would go on—I wonder often about such things—it's such a friendly thing— being human.

Tuesday, January 25, 1938

Hello! To all awful things there must come an end—test week is over! Hooray! We had a Geometry test yesterday—*et** sur- prise (!) I got 94!—which is marvelous for me!!!

> [*Pasted in from the school paper:*] We are interested in the following people at Greeley because their Otis [IQ] tests showed them to have unusual abilities.
>
> Do you suppose our future famous men and women are on this list?
>
> The names follow in the order of the rank made on the Otis tests:
>
> Arnold Wolf, Joan Wehlen . . . [*handwritten by Joan's name:* "me!"]

Mrs. Pfingst collected and inspected the Latin book— I'm afraid she doesn't appreciate the way I fold up pages of books while thinking. One girl was fined 15¢ for chewing (or

---

*Joan often uses Latin for simple words, such as "and" in this sentence.

31

something like that) the cover of her book—I was lucky to get off without a fine.

Wednesday, January 26, 1938

[At the party] we saw Mr. Pfingst—he attracts me—[Mrs. Pfingst] won't be in Greeley next semester, she's taking a vacation and anyhow we wouldn't have her in any case. We'll miss her—after a year and a half, we have grown used to matching our wits with hers—a worthy opponent is a great refreshment—it sharpens one's wits and makes one cleanly work. It's like testing a fine mettled sword with one of equally good steel—sharp and clean in blows. Mrs. Pfingst has meant something to us and has given something to us that we will not forget—*Skål! Skål!**

Tuesday, January 27, 1938

Mrs. Messinger said she needed a girl like me all the time and Mrs. Topping hastily said that I was flighty and always late. Hmm. Flighty. And I always thought of myself as the dignified type. Anyhow we finally finished and were almost the last out of the school. Poor Mrs. Topping. She looks pretty tired nowadays—but oh—she's beautiful. So blonde and straight-browed—like Siegfrieda (her name is Frieda) or someone or Brunhilda. She looks like the Lorelei or some fairy tale princess. Lorraine and I went out of the school slowly then and, oh, the emptiness of the halls. I remember how crowded they were when I first came to Greeley and how frightened and awed we all were. And now they looked so long and still. We went into 102—the first room I had—where I had gone the

---

*Swedish for "cheers."

first day with all the kids so long ago. So long ago. The posters for Latin that we saw the first day were still there:

"These words are derived from Latin. . . ."

. . . So long ago . . . I went over to the seat where I used to sit—next to last in last row. I was a freshie then—oh happy days (daze?). I've had Latin three semesters in that room—I go and the posters remain—how long?

Porto, portare, partavi, portatus.*

How often has that mythic rhythm put me to sleep—how often have I stared out the window during the dear declinations and conjugations—how often has Mrs. Pfingst matched her wits with mine in clean combat? Nevermore, ah, nevermore. Never is such a long word. But it is true. No place can ever be to me what this place—my school—has been. Never means never, nevermore. What remains of me in this school? A carved *J.W.* upon the desk in a few rooms—a name upon my locker—that is all. I saw a picture of a room at Eton where boys had studied Latin for 600 years. Names of Shelley and Pitt† were carved on the seats. Will people conjugate *porto* and *amo* 600 years from now in Greeley, when I am gone so long? Nevermore, ah, nevermore.

Then we went thro' the halls and left our footsteps echoing clear and empty behind us—"Farewell to Greeley—farewell, farewell."

Saturday, January 29, 1938

Have you ever looked right into the eyes of someone you never saw before and will probably never see again and got the queer

---

*The four principle parts of the Latin word meaning "to carry."
†Percy Bysshe Shelley, the English Romantic poet, and William Pitt, prime minister of England in the late 18th and early 19th centuries.

feeling that you were both fellow-dwellers in the world—both human beings? On the streetcar I did—for a minute. I was sitting in the middle of the car and a grey-eyed man was standing in front. For a moment we looked right inside each other and I got the funny feeling described above. He had grey, questioning, calm eyes, and I looked until I remembered I was civilized and dropped my eyes. Then it happened again. Longer and I dropped my eyes again. Then he got off the car. You know the trouble with us is that we really look at each other too seldom. I haven't ever looked at anyone I know that way and only once or twice have I looked into anyone— always someone passing by—or on the same car—always transitory—always. But those people I have looked at I know better than those I have spoken to for years. "The eyes are older than the tongue."

Wednesday, February 2, 1938

English teacher liked the wording of my theme and asked who wrote it. I raised my hand and she looked disappointed. I wonder why. . . .

I had two cards instead of one to fill out in study day before yesterday and on the spur of the moment wrote "John Wheland" on one and handed it in with my own. Today she called out Johnnie's name and no one answered, but she assigned a seat for him anyway. What next?

There was the handsomest boy(s) in my Latin class and most of the kids in Geometry are even dimmer than me—goody.

Sunday, February 6, 1938

Church today—then this afternoon we went to St. Chrysostom's for candle lighting service. All we got to eat was tea and cheese sandwiches—cake. All I eat is cheese nowadays—I feel like Limburger.*

The stars were awfully bright tonite but I still cannot find the newly risen Venus.

Home again, and Mom and I talked philosophy (against her will). We decided (or I did) that nothing really existed, so I didn't do my Latin homework—nice philosophy, that.

I dreamed again last night about a war. I dreamt we were all saying that we would never enter another war and suddenly someone said, "Of course, we will—our brothers will go to the war as their fathers went and it is we that will send them." And we seemed to know she was speaking truth. And I saw the brothers of Vera going to war—because if there were a war they would go—as would everyone. Why do I dream of war—war—war?

Well, it's pretty late.

Good Night!

P.S. Handsome altar boy said, "Hello, Joan," to me today.

Tuesday, February 8, 1938

Surprise! I actually got a seat in art. You see, we have high stools and there aren't enough to go around so I stood. Then Mort said, "Would you like to sit down?" and I just stared and he handed over his chair to me. The whole room stopped working and stared, too. Such gentlemanly behavior is unusual for our school.

---

*Limburger cheese is quite smelly.

Thursday, February 10, 1938

"*Proximi sunt Germanis qui trans Rhenum incolunt, quibuscum semper bellum gerunt.*" That's from Caesar and it means the Germans and Gauls (French) were always fighting. And imagine, Caesar wrote that [in] 58 BC and it's still true today. Makes you kinda think, doesn't it?

Sunday, February 13, 1938

The United States (mine), England and France—the three great democracies as the paper glaringly puts it—sent a note to Japan last week demanding that she cut down on her navies—and yesterday the note came back with an answer— "Go to it—let's have a naval race"—or to the point. And then Thursday night they had a program on the radio discussing the next war in confident tones. Somehow everything seems to point to 1940 as the turning point—as the time when the climax is reached. Everyone seems sure that there will be a war soon. I was talking to a boy in school Friday about war and death. He seemed sure that there'd be another war (another, oh!) and he said he'd probably be killed in it. All the boys I know will be old enough to die in a war in 1940. When I said, "And afterwards—?" he said, "Well, if there's anything to see—afterwards—I'll see it, and if not, well, I won't know about it." Which is, after all, the only thing to say. But think 1940—death—war—oh, why must it be?

Monday, February 14, 1938

I broke an all-time record for coming to school late—I came in at seventh period. You see, I slept late and when I did wake up it was too late to go in the morning so I decided to wait till afternoon. I timed myself so that I'd come during lunch period (I thought—*putavi*) but the periods were temporarily changed so came in in the middle of a period. The hall guard stopped me but after I had explained for about half an hour, she gave a "so-you're-a-freshie" smile and said, "Go in," so I went in. It was my art period and I sneaked in without Mr. Johnston's seeing me. The whole class turned around with a "well-when-did-you-get-here" look and I sunk into the floor. After class I explained (or tried to) to Mr. Johnston, but he has a very suspicious nature—however, he gave in and counted me present—what else could he do—I was there, wasn't I?

Home—radio—homework—journal—bed!!!!

Good night!!!!!!

Tuesday, February 15, 1938

I spoke to the beautiful boy with the uniform in Biology today for 15 minutes. The question that has been worrying all girls in the room I settled—his eyes are blue, not grey. His name is George. Lorraine was very embarrassing—when I walked away from him, she shouted (unnecessarily loudly), "What color are they?" Thoughtless girl. She's beginning to put her books on my hat in the locker again—she ruined my last hat doing that. While I was loudly bewailing that today, Burton came along and comforted me with a "That's nothing—my locker mate sits on mine!" So I don't know which of us is worse off.

Sunday, February 20, 1938

I had a horrible dream about war again last night. In my dream I could see the countries of China and Japan spread out before me on a map.* I could see people milling about in

---

*Joan wrote this entry shortly after the horrific Nanking massacre and mass rapes inflicted on the Chinese by the invading Japanese army.

both countries and in the eyes of the Chinese, in all the eyes, there was a hurried bewilderment and there was a horror in my heart. Someone explained to me what was happening. "The Japanese are too many to fit into their own country so they are sending many of their people over to China." And I could see it happening—the crowds of people hurrying over the narrow strip of water to China and the ever-thickening bewildered crowds in China, hurrying nowhere. "But," I asked, "What will happen to all the Chinese—there are too many!" The answer came—slowly and surely, "They will be killed—deliberately and quickly—every one." And I shouted at my dream, "But they can't do it—they're human beings—the Chinese!" And the words were repeated, "They will kill them—everyone." And an awful horror filled my mind and I saw the people—all of them, hurrying faster—and faster—to nowhere. And faster!

Tuesday, March 1, 1938

March has just come in like a lamb—not exactly a lamb, though—certainly not a lion—maybe a cow—I don't know, it was nice anyhow. I wonder if he will go out like whatever he's supposed to—remember the ides of March—(I just looked upon my March 1 entry of last year and it's exactly the same—haven't I changed at all?). That's marking day this year—isn't that terrible—"Beware the ides of March"—that's the 15th, you know.

Saturday, March 5, 1938

I had another dream about war last night—I dreamt that the Chinese and Japanese were fighting and that I and about 50 other neutral people—white—were behind the Chinese lines. The fighting got worse and worse and we decided to go over to the Japanese lines—but the place between was awfully dangerous. I kept saying, "Oh, go on over—we're sure to die if we stay—we must do something." And I kept thinking it terribly loud, too.

While we were deciding, the Japanese captured the place and conquered the Chinese—we wanted to escape but there was a sentinel at the only free place. So we went to the Japanese commander and asked him to let us go free—when I say "we," I mean I and a few others asked that all 50 might go free. The Japanese commander thought and said, "I will let you all go free on [the] condition that I may kill the last one to leave."

So we left in a hurry and then others formed a line for leaving. We who had left stood around outside the camp to see what would happen—as people will—especially to see who would be the last. One man in the middle of the line deliberately walked back and placed himself at the end— self-sacrifice. I recognized him as a famous doctor-scientist and I thought, "He can't do that—think of what he means to the world. If I were to die, it wouldn't matter so much—I want to be something but I may never be worthwhile and he is already. I will go and place myself at the end of the line." And I believe I actually was going to do so. But other men were at the end of the line—trying each to be last—wholesale self-sacrifice—and as I watched the dream faded—or at least I can remember no more.

I don't know what happened then. . . .

Sunday, March 13, 1938

What a mystical thing this Earth of ours is—what long lands lie on her blue oceans. They all have a triangular form, pointing to the South—to the pole at the end of the world. What law made them so—South America's slim point reaching down to the end of the world. North America's—our continent's— irregular line touching South America. Africa, very like S.A. reaching to the cold South. Eurasia even is in the form of a great sprawling irregular triangle. Even Australia, the lost continent, points vaguely to the South. Only that mysterious Southern continent, Antarctica, where does she point? I used to think of how cruel it was that the Panama Canal should have cut off our continent from South America. I fancied it as a dreadful thing, the separating of two Sister Continents. But how little we do change the Earth after all. I read in the paper today that Germany will annex Austria*—how they'll have to change all the maps and everything—maybe have to buy new maps for Geography classes. But how little we change it. If all men were to die today, would an observer from the moon see any difference? Would it make any difference at all in a thousand years? I wonder.

As I have been writing, the cat has been sitting on the arm of my chair, watching my pen move over the paper. She wonders, I suppose, what useless thing am I doing—moving a black stick over the paper, leaving strange marks on it. She follows the pen with her eyes as I dip it into the ink and back again to the paper to make more black marks on a white sheet—and I watch with her, fascinated. She plays with my pen as it moves and I wonder if I, too, am only playing with

---

*This annexation became known as the *Anschluss* and occurred officially on March 12, 1938. Although this act was forbidden by the Treaty of Versailles after World War I, little was done in the form of protest by foreign governments. In her school notebooks from 1942 to 1943, Joan recorded that one of her teachers "says *Anschluss* was justified morally and economically."

it—making meaningless marks—black meaningless marks. She has jumped down now—tired of my idle sport—wise cat. I wonder. . . .

Then this afternoon I decided to be a good girl and stay home, so Mom and I read—guess what—*Ivanhoe**—and what's more, we actually enjoyed it! We took turns reading aloud to each other and really it was fun—we have to read it for school, you know. The fellow in it I like is Aethelstane in chapter 21; he especially is to my taste—all he thinks about is food—like me. Oh well—here's to *Ivanhoe* and Aethelstane. We just named the cat Aethelstane 'cause she's always so hungry—

Good Night!!!!!!

Sunday, March 27, 1938

Oh, yes. The B.B.B. in B. (beautiful blue-eyed boy in Biology) said, "Hello, Pretty," to me Friday—I'm making headway.

Vera's brother (that usually runs when he sees me) actually said "Hello" to me the other day. But he couldn't see my face so I guess I didn't scare him. That was her big brother. The little brother came over Thursday morning with a note from Vera saying she couldn't come to school, as Mrs. Love was sick. When he came up the stairs, I had one shoe off and my hair in curlers. He stared, gave me the note and ran. Gee, I must have looked awful—

Thursday, April 21, 1938

Last week Vera and I went to Mary's house and I fell in love with her ragdoll, and when the club met there Friday, I found a doll there with a card saying "To Joan Whalen [*sic*]—my

---

*A novel by Sir Walter Scott set in Norman England.

name is Penelope and I am a platinum blonde" and sho' 'nuff Mary really had made one for me—I think that was nice of her.

Sunday, May 1, 1938

Tuesday Mom called me up* and told me I should go to the University of Chicago Saturday for an interview. Was I thrilled! They sent me a pass and I came home Friday—all by myself. I had the nicest ride—two grey-eyed boys sat in front of me.

Yesterday went to [the] University of Chicago with Daddy for interview. It seemed I was the brightest girl and they complimented me and my knees knocked. When they asked what books I had read lately, I couldn't think of anything save *Grimm's Fairy Tales* and *Land of Oz*—finally I blurted out a couple (including Shaw's *Saint Joan* and I said I found the preface more interesting than the play) and they looked pleased. Well, they said it was almost sure that I'd win a $300 scholarship. Gosh! And a chance of renewing next year and for college—oh gosh—

Friday the 13th of May, 1938

Yesterday I handed my English project in—it was a mythology newspaper, rather cute, I must say. "Zeus Sued for Bigamy," "Apollo on Sit Down Strike—Objects to Daylight Savings," "Pegasus Wins Olympic Derby." And I wanted to put "Mercury Freezes" in, but I didn't. I put a picture of Pegasus on it and wanted to paste it in art. I asked Mr. Johnston for paste and, oh gosh, he said he'd paste it for me (he thought it was for art). At first when I explained, I thought something awful was going to happen, but I'm still alive. Mrs. Hellman read

*Joan was on vacation in Wisconsin with her friend Ruth.

42

the newspaper to class and said it was good and showed a fine sense of humour. Hmm? Hmm! That's me!

Good Night!

Monday, May 16, 1938

I've won the Scholarship for the University of Chicago Jr. College.* Am I thrilled! Whoopee!!!!!

Today a girl, Shirley Schuerman, asked *me* to tutor her in *Geometry*! Whew! Was I surprised! However, she seemed serious and I like her so I said I would. She asked me if I'd start tonight at her house, adding that she had a nice brother (do I look like that kind of girl?). So I went over tonight and we did Geometry for 1½ hours. The brother was in some vague upper portion of the house writing a thesis for a Master's degree—he's already completed four yrs at Northwestern—whew! These sweet brothers. I feel awfully inferior. I didn't see him but I saw his picture—he's got grey eyes—!! But the main point is that someone asked *me* to tutor [her] in Geometry! Whoopee!

And of course, that I won a scholarship!

Good Night.

Tuesday, May 17, 1938

Hello! Well, as to my scholarship. It really was funny today. Of course it got around school that I had won it and everyone congratulated me and so forth. But they all seemed so awfully surprised—do I really seem that dumb? And my Geometry teacher, Mrs. Jarvis, heard about it and asked me about it in class. She seemed so dubious about it that I had to laugh. I'm afraid she hasn't a very good impression of me for she went

---

*Now called the University of Chicago Laboratory Schools.

away shaking her head and saying, "I can't understand it." Evidently my Geometry record is not so hot. Mrs. Hellman made me read my letter in class—I blushed so sweetly. . . .

Well, I'm slowly realizing that I've won the scholarship! Do I feel queer. All day people were making cracks. You see, I don't look like the smart type, I'm afraid.

Friday, May 20, 1938

Oh—I'm getting places with B.B.B. in B.* He asked me to go to Riverview† with him in Biology. Let me tell you how it happened.

I was sitting innocently doing my work when he came around and sat beside me (in his uniform—oh!).

Says he: "Have you been to Riverview yet this year?"

Says I: "No—not yet" (gentle hint—that!).

First Annoyance: "Joan, what's the test today going to be on?" (I'm Biology class president and I'm supposed to answer all the questions that come to my desk).

Says I: "Classification."

B.B.B.B.: "Do you like to go to Riverview?"

Second Annoyance: "Hey, Joan, can you give me a pencil?"

Me: "Yes." (Answer to both).

B.B.B.B.: "It's fun to go to Riverview."

Third Annoyance: "Hey, Joan, what's the answer to the third question?"

Me: "I like it." (To B. not Third A.)

B.B.B.B.: "Would you like to go to Riverview?"

Fourth Annoyance: "Hey, Joan, why don't you ever pay me back the paper you owe me?"

---

*Beautiful blue-eyed boy in Biology.

†An amusement park.

Me: "Oh." That was terrible—it might have given B.B.B.B. the wrong impression (he might even think I don't pay my debts!).

Fifth Annoyance: "Joan, what's the idea of all this home-work lately?"

Me (about to fall over): "Oh—hello, Mrs. Sensing." (Don't teachers always turn up at the wrong time? Just as I was getting places.)

Now you see what comes of being President of Biol-ogy class and trying to get places with a soldier at the same time—Oh!

(But we did get places!)

It's fun being president tho'—there's always someone around my desk and it lets you see life from an awfully funny point of view. I had to read the test today and take it at the same time. It wasn't on classification. It was on Reproduction! Forty-one questions for me to read—and answer. Oh gosh. I'd read a question and put it down and answer (if I knew it—usually not) and then look about the room to see a sea of empty faces before me. Usually they saw an empty face before them too.

If I could draw a picture of a blank mind I would, but it seems rather difficult. If one blank mind looked like [this,] would a sea of blank minds look thus:

. . . My conscience is bothering me—every time I talk in third period study, someone gets sent to a corner. (Once I got sent and so obviously enjoyed myself that the teacher wouldn't give me the pleasure again—I stood by a door and talked to all incomers and played myself a game of tic-tac-toe on the wall. What fun.)

And in fifth period study, Laura and I talk steadily and the first time Boris opens his mouth to say, "Be quiet so I can study," he gets sent to the corner. What's become of the "reward of virtue"?

And in art—oh, dear me. Everybody was doing Latin (*pueri**) at my desk and Mr. Johnston came along and scolded everyone else and when I looked up into his eyes (ah!), he didn't say a word to me (I must have scared him).

Tuesday, May 24, 1938

We've got our own telephone†—all our own now, I feel so civilized! Lakeview 7072! That's us: and you don't have to put a nickel in either and it's [the] French type—all in one, you know. Yesterday by some accident while I was waiting for my number, I got another call! (It's a party line.) Quite interesting and unethical.

Well, it happened! He asked me (B.B.B.B.C.‡) again to go to Riverview again! Definitely too—for this Saturday. Gosh, I

---

*Latin for "children."

†Before this, Joan's family had to use a pay phone in the hallway of their apartment building; each call cost a nickel. Then they got their own phone, and the ear and mouth pieces were on one attached handset. They had a "party line," which meant you could listen in on other calls being made in the building.

‡Beautiful blue-eyed boy in Biology class.

hope my appointment at the U. of C.* doesn't get in the way. Should I go with him do you think—(should I—oh gosh!). But the funny part is, I don't particularly admire him anymore. But if I don't go, I'll have wasted three months of admiration.

Sunday I went on [a] bird walk and Dennis and I met by accident (!) on the L† and rode all the way to Jackson Park together. He had a chemistry book with him (he's graduating) and explained to me all about atoms (they're revolving around inside you all the time, just like miniature solar systems) and all sorts of funny things—protons and electrons, etc. It's pretty interesting but I'm glad I'm not taking chemistry.‡ When we got there, we walked down to the bridge and everyone was quite offensive about our coming twice together. But I didn't pitter-pat, as I would have—things always happen too late. Then we rode home.

The city is rather good-looking on Sunday morning from the L—(anytime, [if] you have eyes for it)—spread rather magnificently from the lake far to the west. There is a faery-like quality to the tall sun-smoke-gilded houses, an unreal quality of the people you see moving about in them. The L train passing noncommittally by so many lives, so many stories. If you could walk into one of those unreal houses and puppet-like people, would they be real? Would they be able to speak and feel? Passing on the L, one gets doubts. There are high faery castles down by the lake—apartment houses, you can call them—and in the morning the top is draped in lake clouds. Smoke is a primitive thing, rising from our brick and steel as it rose from forest and grass dwellings of man

---

*University of Chicago.
†The L in Chicago is the elevated train system.
‡Later she married a chemist.

long ago. Who says the city is prosaic? It is the most mystical thing in the world—and the most ephemeral. Our site was a dwelling of wild onions and grass 300 years ago. Who dwells here now—who in another 200 years? Who indeed tomorrow?

Today we had an assembly. A 78-year-old man spoke— German. Very interesting, but I couldn't hear. A teacher, Miss Marsh, died at school. I didn't know her. Mrs. Jarvis was reading the newspaper during assembly. Hitler and Czechoslovakia are having "peace" parlays—who knows? Sunday the newsboys got rid of their extra papers by yelling (in *sotto voce*), "It seems like (*loud*) WAR!" And everyone bought papers— including me—and were fooled.

I'm afraid I'm getting bad in study. One teacher told me yesterday I made everyone around me talk! Hm!

Wednesday, May 25, 1938

We had a Latin test today and I unthinkingly drew pictures of me and Caesar's ghost on it and it was collected. . . . Visited Lewis Institute* Library. Saw historic doors where Mom and Dad met—(oh evil day!) . . .

My feet hurt in art today and I took off one shoe; everyone passed out.

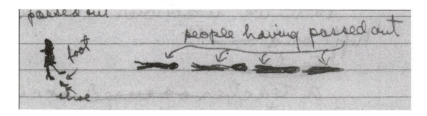

---

*It eventually became part of Illinois Institute of Technology.

Well, I'll give a toast to Woden, Wotan anyhow—perhaps he will be kind to me. I lost my honor bracelet from camp today. My wrist's getting terribly thin and it slipped off.

Sunday, May 29, 1938

Friday night Mom and I went to Lake View to see *Il Trovatore*—given by American Opera Company. Mom went to sleep during it and I had to hold my eyelids up! Are we cultural!

Mom and I went downtown and I got me a new peasant—dusty pink—dress. I look like the *Song of the Lark*[*] or something. It's a dirndl and awfully cute.

B.B.B.B. didn't come Saturday as I told him not to. Vera got walked out on by a boy again. She's going to start using Lifebuoy [soap].

Tuesday, May 31, 1938

Today we were supposed to hand in our Biology notebooks. So in third period, I tried to get some of Gloria's to copy. But I had to pass in my notebook before I got to her. And of course they had to censor everything that passed between us! It was terrible—they cut out all questionable words and read everything and put "Passed" (or "Not Passed"!) by Censor No. I, II, III, etc. Just like Germany! Or Russia or something. A new dictatorship!

It was really awful! And then they got my purse and censored all the junk in that (my lipstick nearly knocked them out), etc. Then the bell rang and I had no work done! Tch! Tch! Tch!

---

[*]A painting by Jules Breton.

P.S. I got tested for T.B. at school today. They punctured you with a needle and wait to see what happens. Thursday I'll know.

Saturday, June 4, 1938

Hello! Well—here goes.

I'm susceptible! That is, to T.B. If I meet anyone who has it, I might catch it. Found that out Thursday 'cause the lump on my arm swelled. They're going to take X-rays of my insides and everything. Gosh, I hope I don't have it! Everybody's joking with me about it—what kind of flowers I want. Very unpleasant.

Miss Sensing called me up to her desk Thursday and gave me a series of the most flattering remarks I ever heard. Wonder if she meant them.

Miss S: "I've been studying your methods."

Me: "Uh—"

Miss S: "I've been trying to copy some of them."

Me: "Uh—"

Miss S: "I've come to the conclusion that you're as popular as you are because you're a good listener. I never see you bursting with what you have to say. You're always interested in the other person."

Me: "Sputter! Sputter!!!"

Miss S: "And how unusual for a girl with your good looks (!), you're as popular with the girls as with the boys."

Me (doubtfully): "Uh-huh."

Miss S: "You have a gift for getting along with people and for leadership. I predict great success in after life (when I'm dead?) for you, etc."

Me (sotto voce): "Give me air!"

Tuesday, June 7, 1938

Sunday night Daddy and I went to Bughouse Square.* Not many talkers there and those not as good as they could have been. One of them was talking anti-everything and while he talked, I saw Venus shining over his shoulder. They say she is blue, but that night she was quite golden. And the man talked, sharply silhouetted against the street lamp, standing on his soapbox, the crowd like some dark elemental mass crowded below him and the great golden orb of Venus over his shoulder. The church spire in the East pierced the sky like a black rapier and the Newberry Library was a gloomy disapproving bulb in the night. It was a picture to take with you, unreal with the insects buzzing in the light and the trees moving like shadows in the warm night. Rain fell for a minute like a canvas over an unreal picture. Grant that I may know more unreal nights like that, when one can half-close one's eyes and seem not to exist at all save as a watcher. Home and the sky was purple.

Everyone's fooling with me about the T.B. test results. As though I'm going to die or something. One boy chants "Joan's got T.B." (which I haven't) all through third period

---

*A nickname for Washington Square Park. Anyone could speak to crowds there, generally on soapboxes.

study. And in art one boy, whom I tried to borrow a piece of art paper from, said, "What do *you* want it for? You won't be able to use it in a little while." Hmmm. And another when I showed him my lipstick, "Huh, you won't be able to use that much longer."

My goodness—I'm getting worried. Gosh!

I sent my registration into U. of C. I chose Biological Sciences instead of Physical. More my line, I think. You need too much brainwork for P.S.

Well—again—Good Night (will you miss me when I'm gone?).

Sunday, June 12, 1938

Well, my name actually got into the paper! Whoops for me. In today's Sunday *Tribune*. You know, June 12 is a sort of anniversary for me. Three years ago the Jolies Amies* (remember them—us) gave the great production of *Naughty Marietta.*† Two years ago today I graduated. A year ago today I got my orange library card saying *"Adult"* on it. So each year June 12 has meant something to me. And this year, I got into the paper! There I am in the Sunday *Tribune*.

> [*Pasted in:*] Another recent Our Town scholarship winner is 15 year old Joan Wehlen, 821 Cornelia Avenue, who is completing her sophomore year at Lake View High school. She won a year's scholarship to the junior college of the University of Chicago.

---

*A club Joan and her pals started. They thought *jolies amies* meant "jolly friends." Of course, it means "pretty friends."
†An operetta that was made into a film in 1935, starring Jeanette MacDonald and Nelson Eddy.

Somehow I seem more like a real person to myself now that my name's in print. I mean, I'm sorta recognized as a human being by the world! So June 12 comes and goes. This week is marking an end to part of my life. That part which dwelt at Lake View is almost done. Before it's time, my high school career is ended and I go forth to new friends, new learning, and new experiences at Jr. College and, because I did not expect to go so soon from Lake View [High School], I did not hold it so close to me. I always thought, "There will be two more years here. I have time." But I did not know. I had not time. So it is with life perhaps. One never expects to go so soon and it is always before you have held it close enough to you. Oh well.

Looking back on my two years in High School—Greeley and Lake View—the moments that stand out in my mind are the quiet ones. The moments that mattered because they mattered so little. The time I stood outside between the school and the portable with the snow drifting down on my bare head I remember. Not knowing where to go (the schedule was irregular), I stood there and the L passed and the snow drifted like pieces of a dream that had no meaning. And then Jimmy Frankel came out and told me where to go. (Not where you think!) It didn't matter, the moment I stood there, indecision in my heart, and the spell was broken when Jimmy came out, but for a moment I was utterly alone in the world and I had a great peace. Such are the moments that really matter. Not the moments with drums and flags and the hot heads. So my high school life is nearly done. One week and this is all. God grant me more such quiet moments in my life, and us all.

Tonight there was a meeting of the Canterbury Guild, and Vera ate supper at my house and then went with me there. Father Young of River Forest was there and I met him and I think I can almost say he's the realest man I ever met. He must be Celtic, Irish or something, at least a bit for there are humorous wrinkles about his mouth and his grey eyes are laughing. He's young and rather good-looking, but it's not that. It's the fun he seems to have living and talking and his slow, quick way of talking that keeps you interested. He's the sort of man you'd like to know anywhere. He told jokes while he was talking and yet his clerical robe seemed to fit him well. After all, religion should be like that—real and humorous.

He talked about . . . the real meaning of Christianity is human contact, being able to get together with other human beings, the going *out* instead of *in* of yourself. And he said that Christ was a perfect example of all those. And he suggested as a motto for the Guild something like that "We should strive to be—" but he wanted us to word it. After others attempted, I tried "Social Christians" and he liked it, so that's it. When he went, he said, "Good-bye, Joan"—he remembered my name. There was a sort of prayer service which we read with him at the beginning and I read the versicals on the third page. So it goes. He was a real man.

Tuesday, June 14, 1938

That is my philosophy: that the act of existence is God and that a rock, no less than an amoeba, no less than a man, is God, because it exists.

Last night I went with [Vera Love's] folks to see Vera dance at a Masonic thing. Amazing. She's a pretty good dancer. Her father kissed her mother when he came home from work. Daddy never does that. I didn't get home till 12—late bird I!

[Five hundred] pages! Oh my goodness! I've written a book!

By the way, I'm a genius. I found out my I.Q. rating accidentally yesterday. It's 141. And the Biology book said people with I.Q.s of 140 or more are "usually considered geniuses." Only 1 percent get that. Maybe I'm the unusual one though— "*qui sabit*"? [One hundred] is normal, you know.

Wednesday, June 15, 1938

One girl had a Dionne quintuplet* doll in art and I had the best time playing with it. Everyone was teasing me about second childhood. Have I passed yet from my first? . . . I've got 500 pages in here now. Isn't that marvelous? I feel so authorish. [Five hundred] is such an important sounding number, like *Ivanhoe* or *20,000 Leagues Under the Sea* or something.

Mrs. Uhlir was telling her class about her son as of old when we came in. Then she made me make a speech to the class about winning the scholarship and embarrassed me very much. She said, "Joanne [*sic*] always did have a flair for writing." I like that, sincerely, really, I mean, you know. 'Cause I want to be a writer. Then we went to see Mrs. Turner who had spread the news of my scholarship all over, and she introduced me to her class and had me blushing and all. All very complimentary.

Except once. When Mrs. Uhlir was bragging about me to the class, she looked at Lorraine who had been standing sorta in background and said, "What are you getting in Geometry?" Lorraine said she was promised an S. Then to me, "And you," confidently. Oh did I feel terrible when I said G. Of course, I may get an E but G is a surer guess.† Anyhow, Mrs.

---

*Canadian quintuplets born in 1934.

†The grades seem to have been E (excellent), G (good), and S (satisfactory).

Uhlir looked quite shocked. And the class grinned its head off (query: does a class have a head?).

Another thing: Mrs. Uhlir told her class I was a smart girl and about the scholarship and all. And all I was carrying was one battered Latin book while Lorraine was loaded down with notebooks and all. You see, *she* does her homework! I'm afraid the class figured that either Mrs. Uhlir had mixed us up or that there is no reward for virtue. So, so. . . .

Thursday, June 16, 1938

Thor's Day this is. No school as it's next to last day. I slept till 12, got up and started to take a bath. While I was comfortably lathering, the bell rang and I got up, dripping wet. Couldn't find bathrobe, put on coat and then it was only Vera.

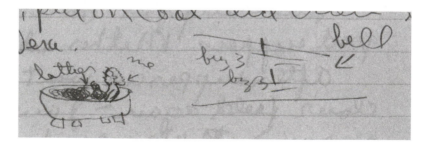

We went to Laura's for club meeting. After supper we went down to the clover field—Jane and Vera and Mary and

I. We were knee deep in clover and danced around in the sweet purple-white field in the night like four ancients in the woods. It was so much fun—"Ring around the Rosy" and everything. Just like little girls again in the dusk.

We played till we were breathless and went on dancing "The Old Grey Mare." We flung ourselves on the grass as we had done in the afternoon.

Oh, in the afternoon it was grand to sink deep into the sweet green and make your own bed of clover. Jane looked so pretty today spread out in the grass.

It's good to get close down in the green till the grass looks like a forest and the flowers are huge and the cool green. . . .

Oh! I found a four-leaf clover today! First time ever. I hope it brings me luck. I put it in my left shoe (that's lucky you know) and now it's all squashed. I'll sleep on it.

Saturday, June 18, 1938

This afternoon we had our Sunday School picnic. I get there hours late. We raced for about four hours, playing sandbag tag, et al. I like to race with the sun behind me and see my long-waisted, slender shadow move across the grass before me with the bobbing hair and low shod foot. It made me feel like a little girl again with the skirt flinging about my knees. As if I'm not a little girl.

Mom and I saw *Snow White* tonite. It's really beautiful. A phrase in a review of it sticks in my mind, "the sad searching fancy of childhood." That does lie in the story. Something with golden dust on it to remember.

Sunday, June 19, 1938

Well, I won first prize for my essay on Martin Luther today! You know, the one I sat up till 2:30 for last Saturday. Well, I won! I was so surprised! It was announced in church and I was sitting in the choir blissfully counting my feet (two of them), when I heard an acolyte whisper, "Joan Wehlen, she's here." And Pat poked me and I got up to receive the prize. It was a book, *Moby Dick*, signed by Father Carr and Mr. Hebley and inscribed "First Prize." So there!

Today was the last Sunday School Sunday of the season. Prizes for perfect attendance given out. Little crosses. Of course *I* didn't get one! Not for perfect attendance. Of the 15 who had perfect attendance so far, only seven were there to receive their prizes. Very embarrassing. You know, I promised to split my prize if I won it with Mrs. Love as she dictated some Martin Luther notes to me, but I couldn't rip up the book, so I guess I keep it.

Midsummer's Day, Tuesday, June 21, 1938

I went swimming with Daddy today. Or at least *I* went swimming. Daddy said he didn't want to get his suit wet, but I suspect he thought the water was too cold. Anyhow, I went into the clear green flowing ice and tingled from head to toe. It's like a release from prison to get into the lake after so long. I'm a lake girl, you know, and there's something inevitable in that the water was green and clear and you could see the white rocks far below. I'm getting so I don't upset the whole lake when I dive now.

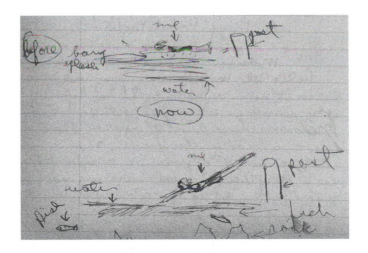

So, you see, I have improved. At least I don't cause a tidal wave when I dive anymore. And no little fish come dead to the surface from the shock anymore. . . .

Wednesday, June 22, 1938

This is Wotan's Day. In the morning I went to *that* place to get X-rays taken for T.B. Met a graduated senior from Lake View there, Vernon Cowan. He reads [P. G.] Wodehouse, too. He said he'd call me up tomorrow, but I didn't give him my telephone number. I wonder how my insides look in the X-ray. I wanted to take it home but they wouldn't even let me see it. It was very awkward—a big machine and then they snap the picture.

Went to the Art Institute for the afternoon. Had [a] lovely half hour contemplating [*A*] *Chemist Lifting with* [*Extreme*] *Precaution the Cuticle of a Grand Piano*. Modern art [by Salvador Dalí]. There was a curly blonde fellow sitting next to me. We both considered the picture for a long time. Then I got up to look again to see I wasn't crazy. I sat down. He got up. Ditto. We looked at each other. A woman came into the room, looked at the picture and started back (it has that effect). Then, thinking we were together, she started to discuss the picture with C.B. [Curly Blonde] and me. No decision, though we nodded solemnly.

Tonight I went to Vera's to sew my dress on her sewing machine. I'm afraid the seams aren't very straight. I sewed up the placket by accident. I'm afraid I wasn't "sewing a fine seam" like the gal in the poem ["Curly Locks"].

Saturday, June 25, 1938

Went out with Daddy tonight. Went [to the] store to get face powder. Daddy said [I] may as well get what else I need for camp in way of beauty junk too. And did I—at least nine other things! You should have seen the look on Daddy's face! He's never going to risk that again.

Saturday, August 27, 1938

Well, here I am again after two months. Have you missed me? I missed you. Many a time I wanted to write something in you and you were not there. But now, looking backward, it is the quiet moments of the summer that stand out in my mind. The last rainy Saturday afternoon when Dennis and I spent the afternoon in Brownie [cabin] playing on the old Victrola—"Liebestraum" and "Going Home" and "Danse Macabre"—all the songs that will stay in my head for the rest of my life—while the rain was pouring down on the roof and the leaves were shivering outside.

How full that afternoon was! First, we all went swimming and it rained and the water was like hard ice. Then we came up the hill in the rain and I had a class of Peppers* in Brownie [cabin] painting star maps. So I went there in my dressmaker bathing suit and watched the class.

Andy and Dennis were in the back room in what they called the "Batchelors [sic] Corner." However they let me join them as I said I was going to be an old maid. So we sat and talked for a while. Then Andy looked at me and said disapprovingly, "Go and put some clothes on, Joan," and I was wearing my bathing suit. And it looked like a playsuit.

But I did as he said. When I came back, the Peppers were almost done, so they went out and I cleaned

*A group of campers.

up Brownie. Then Dennis and Andy and I sat talking for a while. Then Andy went and Dennis and I sat talking. Then we played the Victrola while it rained.

Funny, but for three years I have come home with the same dream in my heart. I've got it yet. It's still Dennis Turner.

See, it is the quiet moments that you remember.

I remember so many things; I cannot write them all out.

I remember the day Bump and Kennelly and I sat in Brownie and discussed Andy thoroughly only to discover that he was in the backroom ostentatiously sleeping. Oh, how I laughed, for I was the only one who hadn't said I like him.

All the funny moments that stay in my mind. The time I wrote to Richard Forney "Please send a package of gum to Miss Joan Wehlen, Arden Shore Camp, Lake Bluff, Ill."—and he did it! Oh, did I laugh! And then I wrote a "thank you" and started down the road to mail it and Dennis called me, "Joan" (how beautiful that name is now!) and caught up with me and we went up the road together. O. Henry says somewhere that life is but a road with two walking up it—together.

And it was such a glorious golden day! Just as we got to the end of the road, the bell rang and I looked at him and said, "Oh, will I have time to mail my letter?" and he said, "I'll mail it for you." And he did and I walked slowly to the dining room. And I just laughed and laughed 'cause it said Richard Fornay on the envelope. Hah hah!

All the quiet days remain in my mind. The time Beverly and I and Dennis and Norman Turner went butterfly hunting together. I rather liked Norman then, so we paired off with one net and cyanide bottle and butterfly net and they took the other. We went deep into Skokie Valley, and it was a glorious day with the bergamot and goldenrod in bloom and the grass high and the sun golden and the sky blue with white clouds. On we went (how romantic) and caught butterflies and ate all the poisonous looking things we could find. Norman and I went down to a swamp filled with white flowers to pick some red berries and almost fell in! And at that, the berries were bitter. Then he and I went up to get some apples and, in going down a hill, walked right into a hawthorn tree. Finally we found the apple tree and he climbed it and threw the apples down to me and I put them in the butterfly net. Then we discovered a pear tree with tiny hard green pears and he got some of those and then we lay down in the deep grass under the pear tree and tried to eat them. Very difficult.

By that time Dennis and Beverly had caught up with us (they had been chasing butterflies—imagine!) and lay down with us and attacked the pears. Then while the sun made patterns on the grass, they taught us how to play on grass. And we lay back and blew on the grass. It really makes a beautiful sound. Finally we gave up the pears and decided to catch some butterflies (or they did!). So we went on again and came to a huge field filled with bergamot and goldenrod. We tried to catch some butterflies but finally we gave Bev our net and she and Dennis went after a tiger swallowtail.

We couldn't do anything so we lay down in the deep grass under a low tree at the edge of the field. That is, I did and Norman said, "Nice place you picked out," and joined me. Then we lay and discussed all sorts of things and the grass was deep and a spider was considering us. It was so romantic—like Omar Khayyam.*

A bottle of cyanide beneath the bough
A couple of spiders and thou
Sprawling beside me in the wilderness
Oh wilderness were paradise enow!

Isn't that beautiful? That's just how I felt too.

Finally we got up and looked for the others, and guess what—they were gone! After some fool butterfly, I suppose. Anyhow, Norm said he knew the way home and, though I

---

*The following poem is Joan's parody of the medieval Persian poem *The Rubaiyat of Omar Khayyam*, translated by Edward Fitzgerald. The original reads: "A Book of Verses underneath the Bough, / A Jug of Wine, a Loaf of Bread—and Thou / Beside me singing in the Wilderness— / Oh, Wilderness were Paradise enow!"

was sure it was in the opposite direction, I followed him. I felt like one of the babes in the wood* or something. Then (us nature students) we started to give flicker calls and guess what happened. A pewee answered! How embarrassing! Then we were answered once by a fake sounding pewee and we decided it must be the other two. And it was. So we walked back to camp very thirsty and tired. When we got back and we went to Boyville fountain for a drink and I leaned over to drink, guess what happened! Dumb me! The cyanide bottle slipped and broke and all the deadly fumes started rising and it's poison to humans too. So Norman sent for a broom and we swept it outside and so far as I know no one in Boyville has died yet.

(This I am continuing on Friday, Sept. 2, 1938) And all the other lovely quiet days we had. . . .

I seem to be remembering the whole two months now. Everything comes back in quick sunshine dust-flashes. . . . The nights when we went down to the pier star-gazing and saw through the telescope three of Jupiter's moons. Those dreamy nights when the stars were blazing and we stood on the pier while the shoreline stretched away like the misted horizon of another planet. And the night I lectured on stars down there with a cold and the Perseids fell. The shooting stars we saw and . . . suddenly we saw Venus like a blue fire in the west over the trees.

And the night I couldn't sleep when I awoke at 1:30 and lay in Brownie [cabin] looking up at the sky listening to the crickets. Then I got up and stood in the soft night and looked up at Vega while the grass brushed my feet and the insects

---

*A traditional tale in which two children are killed and covered with leaves by birds.

sang. And I thought: we are all going towards her, for all the soft summer night and the singing of the insects, we are all going to Vega.

Saturday, September 10, 1938

I would rather think men are good and err, than think them evil and be right. I would . . .

Wednesday, September 14, 1938

There's war in the air. Czechoslovakia and Germany are having it out over the Sudeten people, etc. Britain, France, Russia with Czechoslovakia and Germany with her new conquest Austria (did I tell you about that?—Germany invaded Austria and now it belongs to her).* Unfortunately, very much like World War. I hope it doesn't come to anything but the newsstands are full of extras. And there was fighting on the border today.

Monday, September 19, 1938

Well, world news goeth on too. See this—"Allies (Britain and France) give in to Germany—leave Czechoslovakia flat!" Czechoslovakia says she'll fight and Germany says it will be a "real" War. I wonder what Hitler said to Chamberlain that made Britain side step so neatly.†

---

*See entry dated Sunday, March 13, 1938.
†Joan pasted into her diary the newspaper clipping on page 67, which depicts Chamberlain and Hitler at the famous appeasement talks about Czechoslovakia. On it Joan wrote, "This is Hitler and Chamberlain conferring—doesn't Hitler look tired?"

Chamberlain Back in London; Await Action by Cabine

[Associated Press Photo: Sent yesterday by radio and wirephoto]

The first picture of historic conference at Berchtesgaden over the fate of Czechoslovakia. Left to right: Prime Minister Chamberlain of Great Britain; Reichsfuehrer Adolf Hitler of Germany, Joachim Nazi foreign minister, and Nevile Henderson, British en-

This is Hitler and Chamberlain conferring— but Hitler looks tired.—

Wednesday, September 21, 1938

Hi ya! This is the autumnal equinox and Daddy's birthday! That's funny, you know, Daddy was born on the autumnal equinox, Mom and Dad were married on the vernal equinox and I was born on about the winter solstice. Aren't we seasonal?

[After a trip to the Art Institute] I boarded one of the old busses—I think I still like them better and seated myself joyfully in the front seat. The window was open and I inhaled the dying summer. A young man in a brown suit sat next to me.

Suddenly!!!—I looked down at my skirt—! There was a brown thing with six legs crawling on it (not a cockroach!!) somewhat like this:

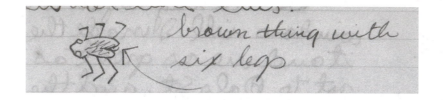

I yelped! And hastily tried to brush it off. It stuck. Maybe my plaid skirt had attracted it. I got out an envelope and shoved it under the bug. The bug was stubborn. By this time the young man was watching interestedly. I got the bug on the envelope and deposited him on the front windowsill. I relaxed and settled back. Then suddenly—the bug flew! It had wings! From the front windowsill to the one beside me it flew. I jumped and moved closer [to] the y.m. [young man]. He was smiling sympathetically. Thus we were.

The bug began to crawl along the windowsill. I made the space between it and me as great as possible. We got to Oak St. and the bug had advanced and was now crawling up the windowsill. I relaxed and considered that incident over; I looked at the lake. It was blue grey and the waves were high and white. The long shadows of the skyscrapers lay on the sand—the white roaring foam brushed at them.

Suddenly, a whirr of wings, a breath across my face and the six-legged thing touched me. I jumped and landed slightly on the young man's knee. I eyed him and the bug, murmured, "Excuse me," and returned myself to the seat—still keeping the distance between me and bug as great as possible. The y.m. was now openly grinning. I kept my gaze fastened on the bug—I wasn't taking any second chances. It moved and seemed about to fly. I moved in direction of young man. Bug considered. I gulped.

Young man suggested (delightful drawl!), "Why don't you brush him to the floor and step on him?" Now, you know I have scruples about killing things and anyhow I didn't fancy touching it, but didn't want to discuss the morality of destroying insect life with said y.m. So I said, "No, I think I'll leave it there—!" He said, "Is it a fly?" And I answered, my eye still on it, brightly, "I don't know—it's got wings." And we both silently considered the brown thing with six legs. On to Diversey. The bug was crawling up the windowsill. Belmont—he had reached the top. Melrose—he was gone! Where was he? I look about frantically. He was on my skirt! I yelped, "Oo!' and we both gazed down. I started hastily to brush it off, but it landed on my leg.

And those old-fashioned busses are made so you can't lean over in the seat. I could feel its six legs walking on me and moved uneasily. I think it fell off. I leaned back, still picturing the thing on my leg. We stared out the window. Addison. I got off—leaving bug and young man behind me forever. . . .

P.S. Well, for the time, war is averted.

Monday, September 26, 1938

I listened to Hitler's speech in Germany. As I "non speak Deutsch" (that's three languages there!) I didn't understand, but an announcer translated at intervals. Saturday is scheduled for the invasion of Czechoslovakia if the Checks [sic] don't give in. We'll wait.

Thursday, September 29, 1938

Well—our mythical "peace" is again floating over the land of Europe while four statesmen pretend to come to an agreement.

The headline says, "War Averted"—but I know—it should say "War Postponed"—*I know*.

Hell to—with—politics.

Monday, October 3, 1938

Well, I've started at University High! I got there late as usual but I've resolved—never again.* It was all on account of the L, you see. The Jackson Park Express doesn't stop at Belmont in the morning—only I didn't know that. Waited patiently, the L came . . . I brightened up . . . L passed by . . . I stormed up to guard who was already explaining to an irate young man. He told us what L to take to Chicago Ave. We got on very crowded train. Finally reached Chicago Ave. Me and irate young man (no longer irate) got off. We were way at the end of funny platform. We began to walk, slowly, puzzledly. Did you ever walk in perfect harmony, without talking? We did. Finally L came. Got on. He got off the stop before me. I was 15 minutes late.

Sunday, October 9, 1938

Met Lorraine. Says she:

"Oh, I miss you at school, Joan!"

Me (flattered): "Why?"

She: "Laura hasn't a hat."

You know, she always used to lay her books smack on my hat—now she says she hasn't the heart to lay them anywhere. Hum! Hum! Oh well, remember the time I spilled Higgins Eternal Ink all over her artwork. "It'll never come off," she mourned, and I remember I pictured it eternally splattered on

---

*Almost every subsequent entry about school indicates she was late.

that piece of paper, though nations arose and fell—Higgins Eternal—forever!

Thursday my mate in Biology and I (not my real mate you know—just my microscope mate) discovered two whirlpool things in a mess of green slime in our microscope. They were like this:

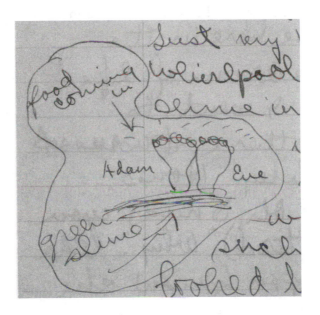

You see, they can't go out for their food, so they make a whirlpool and throw it in. It seemed such an idyllic life and the slime looked like a pretty garden so we named them Adam and Eve! Then we went out to lunch and when we came back they had evaporated. Query: "What had happened to Adam and Eve?"

We were quite worried about them.

I dreamed I was Hitler last night. Only I was me, too—I mean, I didn't change shape. At first I was watching him and suddenly I became him. It seemed I (him and me) was going to be assassinated and I had to run. I got out and ran in the rain while the conspirators followed me. It was in Berlin— and raining. The streets seemed empty. A cab came along and I got into it. The cabby was quite nice, only he didn't believe I had any money. I showed him. He drove around. Then the conspirators came along searching for me. They looked in the cab and I hid on the floor under a sheet. They thought I was a corpse and came around to investigate.

While they were coming (which took an inordinately long time), the cabby and I slipped out and ran to his house, which was conveniently on the same street. He must have been a nonrevolutionist for he said he'd help me escape. We packed a lunch and, while the conspirators were coming up, slipped out the front way. There were two bicycles there which seemed to be for us, so I took one. We dashed out in the rain and had gone a little way when we met a student there. I saw the cabby didn't have a bike. It seemed he hadn't known they were there, though it was very dangerous. We ran back for it. The front lobby was now a library, but we got in, got the bike and slipped out, apparently unnoticed. Then we rode alone—hunched our shoulders in the rain through the empty streets of Berlin for about two blocks and Momma woke me up. Wasn't that disgusting?

Monday, October 10, 1938

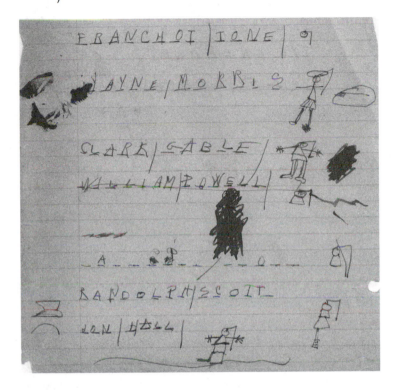

Wednesday, October 12, 1938

Hiya! Well, my article "Vox Pop" in the *U-High Midway*[*] got printed Friday in a nice prominent place and I'm due to write another tomorrow.

Very embarrassing incident in art today. We were seeing movies on Egyptian art and I was sitting next to lovely boy

---

[*]The school newspaper at the University of Chicago Laboratory High School (U-High).

named Bruce (funny, I always make more headway in movies—can it be my looks?) and the teacher was talking about symbolic poses of things in Egyptian art—kings, etc. And then she says, "And children were always pictured with their fingers in their mouths—like over there"—pointing to me and Bruce who hurriedly removed our hands and hid them under the table, feeling very puerile!

Well, had to translate eight lines of Latin poetry for Humanities tonight. Very gloomy—all about "death conquers everything—the mountains fall over and nothing is left for a long time"—boo hoo.

Sunday, October 30, 1938

I have decided: I shall marry a cave man—a meat-eater—one who lives *venationibus* (by hunting). We didn't have meat today (darn the fiends!) and about two o'clock I started talking about Roger Bacon; three o'clock Charles Lamb;* four o'clock I was discussing heatedly the superiority of the cave man's existence—"The Simple Life." Then suddenly Mom said, "I know why she's talking like that. She's hungry." I had just finished saying "When the cave man was hungry he went out and killed his food." Me for the cave man! [Later I read] all about cave men—Neanderthals, etc. And there were pictures of them all. And suddenly I saw how I wouldn't want to marry a cave man—he recedes too much—receding forehead, receding chin—everything recedes—thus:

---

*Roger Bacon is the medieval English philosopher; Charles Lamb wrote *Tales from Shakespeare* with his sister, Mary, in the early 19th century.

74

You know how I had decided to marry a cave man because they lived naturally—you know—killed when hungry, etc. Well, suddenly he didn't seem right for me. I turned to the man next to me and it relieved me to see he had a chin, etc. No receding. He wasn't very beautiful, but compared to the receding Java Ape man, his homeliness was beautiful. I could have hugged him for that he had a chin. But I controlled myself. I looked out at the street and suddenly I felt proud of my beautiful slender strong-chinned race. Seeing the people erect and hairless in the streets, I was proud to be one of them—not a receding cave man.

I saw the buildings jutting their dim hulls into the sky and the grey sidewalks and the long chimneys and the bridges and the tracks. And I thought, "All this we have made with our hands—these things have we built ourselves. And the only real thing here is the river. There it was dim and elemental, but there it had been when there was no stone to bind its course." I knew then that, though the cave man had lived a simpler life, I could not live his life. This was my life, of sidewalks and buildings and great roaring engines. Artificial but natural to me. I was a bit proud then as I looked at Neanderthallus and Java Ape man. I was proud of my strong, slim chin and of the man's next to me and of the erect slender people in the street, unafraid of the roaring engines. There was no tree in sight—nothing that was real save the river—bound by cement. This was my time—my race.

Then I turned the page and came to Cro-Magnon man. And all my pride fell down a heap. For he was not only full-chinned and foreheaded, but there was strength as well as intelligence in his face. Something thus:

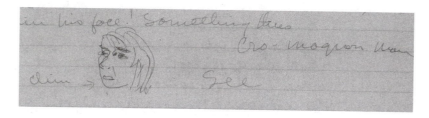

I felt humbled before him. It said in the book I read, that he was perfect physically, six ft. tall, etc. And his brain capacity was larger than man's today. And he had such a puzzled, eager, questing look on his face. I could read a soul into it. I read in the book "with Cro-Magnon our physical evolution ceased and now has begun to decrease." I looked at the man. So we have traded our hands for our hearts, I thought; and yet are our hearts any greater than his? He was perfect—physically—but who, looking at his strong, intellectual face—can say modern man is superior in any way? I say not only physical, but also mental evolution ceased with Cro-Magnon. He has such a wonderful questing look on his face. It is true that we question also, but it seemed to me his question is the greater. The answer to our questions would not be as great as is the answer to his. He asks why, we only ask how. Or such I read in his face.

It seems to me that he, Cro-Magnon, achieved the perfect balance of life—between body and mind—physical and mental. We have lost that balance. Neanderthallus never had it. We have lost our bodies and cultivate mind. Cro-Magnon balanced those. His was the true life—and yet he was a cave man. Would there were such a cave man today! And yet, though I know this thing, I cannot live his life. He had the perfect balance but my race has lost it. We have over-balanced ourselves. His was the peak of humanity—we are on the downgrade. And I cannot stop it. It is evolution. And suddenly the white hands on my lap were distasteful to me and my books that had no meaning were hateful to me.

Then I went back to the difference between man and animals. Very slight, it seems. I was testing myself out to see if I was human. Seeing if my thumb was opposable (by wiggling it) and if I had definite chin (thrusting it out) and if my great toe was opposable (very hard in shoes). By this time, the man next to me also seemed to need proof that I was human and took quite an interest in my experiments. In most points I seemed human so I gave up and went back to one-celled animals. Man went back to his magazine.

Somehow the next person's book always seem more interesting than your own. (Ever notice that?) So I started to read his magazine—he was reading article entitled "Morality Among Modern Youth"—and he started to read my Bio book. Subject: Reproduction in One-celled Animals (or plants or something). Then when the other's article got too deep we shifted and went on with our own—very convenient cooperative effort.

All very complicated . . .

Did I tell you we went to see *Faust* at the auditorium last month (25¢ last row in gallery)—Man kept selling ice-cream bars in intermission—very unoperatic. I liked Mephistoph-eles though! Am going to name my next plant that—Eurydice is dead, you know. She shed all her leaves. Poor Eurydice!

I wish someone wanted me. Penelope [my doll] loves me and Tristan [my plant]. Good night.

Friday, November 4, 1938

Hello! Well—guess what? We studied bread mold today—just before lunch too. It's all gushy and green and full of spores and reproduction and all (biology is so indelicate).

Then I'm supposed to ask the leading boys of the school what their ideal girl is in life for "Vox Pop" next week. You know, I run the "Inquiring Reporter" column in the *Midway*—every week—four weeks so far. Some of the columns are pretty cute. This week was the "ideal girl." In connection with my column, I asked Orville (him with the mus-tache) if he was a leading boy—he looked so embarrassed and modest and all, but he's on the track team.

Wednesday, November 9, 1938

I got to school early this morning. . . . I planted myself in front hall and pounced on everyone who came in saying, "Describe your ideal U-High girl." One of them wanted a "glamorous blonde with a slinky walk." Hmmmm.

Monday, November 14, 1938

After lunch I went to teachers' lunchroom to ask questions for "Vox Pop"—"What's your idea of an ideal pupil?"—teachers all male. Mr. Heaton says one who brings apples every morning. I shall remember that sometime. Mr. Trumpell asked me if I wrote the column every week—he said he got a kick out of it—especially my terse remarks, says he. (I looked up "terse" in the dictionary; it means, "elegantly and forcefully concise"—that's me!). I had to get my picture taken for *Cosmopolites** today. Sorta sickly smiles on faces of all.

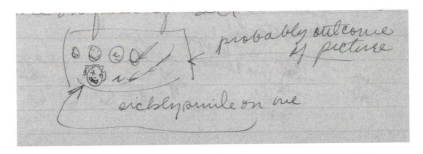

Monday, November 21, 1938

And then today—oh, today was a lovely day. In the morning from the L, the world was real and tangible in the bright air and the sunlight. Then when I got to school (one minute on

---

*Evidently a club for those who are cosmopolitan.

time), I walked into AP 1 and the boy behind me started to tell me how what Mr. Heaton said for my column brought results—You know for his "ideal pupil," he said one who brings apples every day. Well, it seemed every one in the school took the hint, for there was Mr. H. with apples, apples, apples of all kinds on his desk—big, little, even one with a ribbon on it. Well, it proves someone reads the column, as my editor cynically said. In the middle of the class during organization paper writing, Mr. Heaton came up to me and said, "Well, I suppose you want your share of the loot." And I said, "Oh, of course! I expect my commission." And he grinned and said to take my pick. So at lunchtime Bobby Smith and I went up and took some big red apples while Mr. Heaton grinned (he's so cute!) and Richard Schindler looked puzzled. As I explained, it will stop the Depression—fruit stores sell more, pupils get A's, Mr. Heaton gets fat and I get my commission.

Tuesday, November 22, 1938

Yesterday as I came on the L, I saw the reflection of the interior of the train in the night and, seeing it so real, yet truly so intangible, I wondered if all life were not such—apparently real, yet slipping beneath us if we try to step hard on it. We passed a station and the man beside me seemed in the reflection to be looking over a real woman's shoulder on the station, and yet they were really utterly separate and unconscious of each other. And suddenly I thought, perhaps that is the other dimension. Who is looking over your shoulder now, Joan?

Today I was just about to get the fourth dimension explained at lunch by a very handsome fellow when Bruce came up and distracted me until it was all over. Now I'll never know what the fourth dimension is. . . .

Who knows to what I shall come? Remember this day, Joan.

Thanksgiving, Thursday, November 24, 1938

I went to church like an honest girl today and—oh—guess
what??? Remember the grey-eyed choirboy I used to rave
about—Paul Kappe—? Well, I was walking home from church
with Bob M. and his brother when, guess what? He caught up
with us. Well, you know, I've been like that for about two years
but anything deadens in time and I had just about forgotten
about *him*. And then there he was. Then we walked along for a
while and I started to turn down Cornelia. *He* said he thought
he'd go that way too to get to the L. Well, any fool knows you
can't get the L on Cornelia as Bob forcefully pointed out to my
great disgust. Nonetheless, he persevered and came after me.

Oh—what a lovely two blocks. We talked about things
and all—and he said, "You're one of my sisters, aren't you?"
(his mother is my godmother) and I said, "Yes, sorta," and
he said, "I know, I've been making inquiries," and I gazed
sweetly at the sidewalk. And then we talked about adopting
sisters and brothers and I said I'd like a brother about five
ft—uh. Says he, "Eleven," and I said uh-huh (he's about that)
with grey eyes. "But I've got cat's eyes," he objects. [We argue
whether or not he] looks like Errol Flynn.* "Well, I still think
I do," he says. Then unfortunately we got home and I had to
go up. I rang the bell about 25 times and said, "Whoopee,
the handsome choir boy walked home with me." After hearing about said crush for two years, you can imagine how this
affected the family. (P.S. In walking with him I was careful
to keep my toothless side away. It's terrible to teeth so late.)

Then we had Thanksgiving dinner and spent afternoon
and evening fooling around and pretending we were cave

*Errol Flynn was a movie star Joan found handsome. She even cut a
picture of him out of the newspaper for her scrapbook.

men having to talk in sign language punctuated by grunts (my idea—effect of Humanities). (Remember when we played Kentucky mountaineer and King Alfred and Lady Guinevere?) Well, Daddy was Chief Mud-in-the-Face, Mom was Lump of Fat, and I was Blockhead (later the Sylph-like Faun). Well, so goeth Thanksgiving. . . .

Monday, December 5, 1938

Art today—during movies on Greek Art, B. and I got to the handholding stage, but I'm too restless I guess and can't take it. He had to take a test then on Aegean art. Well . . .

Tuesday, December 6, 1938

Question of the week is "Describe your ideal teacher." Mr. Heaton offered to pay me "hush" money.

Wednesday, December 7, 1938

Bruce rushed up to me in the corridor today and said, "Oh, Joan, I've been looking all over for you—I want to ask you something!" And I got all thrilled and so forth and then guess what—he says, "Do you still want that talk in Art?" (Miss Lee had given him a talk on Greek Archaic art which I had wanted) and I said yes and he gave it to me—Great letdown of the season.

We had a test in Humanities today—Semitic history—I've got a theory of history—"all the invasions come from the North"—so far the history books agree. Is it Canada for us?

Obituary: Mom seems to have thrown out all my old mementoes—the pin B.B.B. in B. gave me—the acorn ring Dennis made for me that summer—my honor pin that I had for three semesters at Lake View—all the old memories. My Latin Classical League pin—everything. I've got no place of my own to put things. I thought that now I'd won the scholarship, they'd try to make it easier for me, but that doesn't seem so. It seems harder all around. Here and there.

I need a room or at least a desk to study on—as it is, I have to wait till the kitchen table is cleared and dishes done to even get any quiet to get started (and then I have steady interruptions) and that's usually about eight o'clock: 1½ hours for homework. 9:30: Bath, wash clothes, put up hair. 10:30: Write here. 11:00: To bed. Then get up at six. That gives me seven hours sleep, if there are no hitches—and there usually are. Then when I have nature study classes or choir, it's even later. And that gives no time for recreation—grant us thy peace. And the cool earth sounds sweet. . . . How about advertizing in the paper—"Wanted—one room to study in—Please apply Joan Wehlen"—Oh and I do need it—!!

I've already lost 1½ pounds and Dr. Downing says I'm 7½ pounds underweight. I got measured today.

Tuesday, December 13, 1938

Suggested a new column for the paper—"Aunt Polly Answers"—you know, a sort of advice affair—only supposedly humorous. This week's "Inquiring Reporter" question is, "What do you want for Christmas?" I want my cottage, some sleep—a great deal of it—and Sir Grey-Eyes. House of Happiness* class going to Christmas party next week. On my birthday too—the 20th.

Gee, I'll be 16 then. How will that feel, I wonder?

Fifteen is a lovely age—close enough to life to watch it and to have the wind of it stir your hair but not too close. I shall

---

*Now known as Benton House, it was founded in the early 20th century. By the time Joan worked there, it offered classes for children in various activities such as sewing, sports, and the arts.

be sorry to leave 15 and become 16. It sounds so old. . . . Only seven days of 15 left. I'm almost an old woman.

Woden's Day, Wednesday, December 14, 1938

I was chosen to be Mary for our Christmas pageant! Oh I'm so happy! It's to be this Sunday. She told me at Choir practice tonight.

Tonight Daddy and I went over that little Swedish children's bible stories book we found. I'm OK at Swedish for a beginner. I think I'll try to learn it. Daddy sounds so unnatural translating with unfamiliarity the Lord's Prayer. But the words of some of those things are great on any tongue.

Freya's Day, Friday, December 16, 1938

I had the horriblest experience today. I think I ate a worm—yes, a worm. A squirming one. You see, I bought a package of peanuts to eat in Bio Sci[*] (before class—of course) and, just as I reached the bottom, I found Mr. Squirmus Squirmorus there. Sort of curled up in a ball, you see. Hurriedly removed him from mouth and spent rest of period wondering whether I had eaten his wife and family who very likely also inhabited peanut package. Which brings to mind [a] joke about "What's worse than finding a worm in an apple you've been eating?"—Answer: "Half a worm." When I told Barbara and Pat at lunch, they wouldn't let me eat anything else, claiming I was on a "Diet of Worms" and I didn't catch on for the longest time—until I remembered Martin Luther and howled. And howled.[†]

---

[*]Biological science (which is also referred to as "Bi Sci").
[†]The Diet of Worms was an assembly that took place in Worms, Germany, in 1521. It dealt with Martin Luther and the Protestant Reformation.

Saturday, December 17, 1938

You know I'm the Madonna and I sit there in front with a white kerchief on my head, surrounded by all the little angels. There was a straw-filled manger beside me. And suddenly I felt ashamed of myself and silly and good and enjoyed rehearsing it. Just as I was about to leave, my Joseph came and we had to rehearse once together in the dark church. He's Cameron Brown. It's all very beautiful but the rehearsal was terrible.

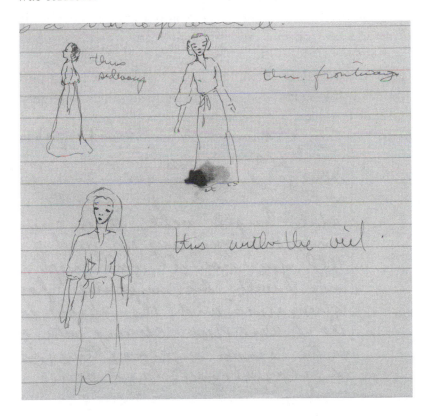

Sunday, December 18, 1938, 3:00

Oh, I've been the Virgin, sitting in blue gauze with a veil on my head, watching the manger. And the little white angels with their candles were surrounding us and I cannot tell you how it was. Joseph behind me with his impassive face and strong arms, and the shepherds and the Wise Men coming with gifts for the empty manger (there was only a flashlight and some straw in the manger).

But I cannot tell you how happy I am.

First the angels arose singing and then the shepherds came and saw the star. And then she read—"and Mary and Joseph went forth into Bethlehem"—and while they sang "O Little Town of Bethlehem," he and I walked slowly out and around, I sinking at the stair. Then more singing and angels, and they move apart to reveal me and the manger.

"And they found Mary and Joseph and the Babe lying in a manger." And all the little angels came up to peer into the manger and so forth.

Then "Silent Night" and all the sudden I felt so strange sitting there with the soft white angels and Joseph's low voice all singing around me—and the light shining from the crib. Wise men and shepherds to watch. How did the first Mary feel? Then when it came time to go, the little angels didn't go. I was absolutely thoughtless and couldn't think of a thing. But Joseph whispers, "When the music stops, we'll go out and they'll follow." So he helped me up and we went slowly out with the little white angels following. All over then and I was so happy. Afterwards, I went into the chapel and gave thanks all alone in the dark.

It's so wonderful to be the Virgin Mary and almost 16 and so awfully happy on a cold bright winter day.

Tuesday, December 20, 1938

Well, here I am, 16, and I don't feel much different. Just a little. Though Gladys and Jane and Mary and Ruth came over and we had a sort of party. I look in the mirror and I think, "I'm 16." I ride on the L and I think, "I'm 16." But I haven't had much time to think all day—two tests and one coming tomorrow.

But mostly I'm 16; the mystic age, 16. Joan Wehlen, 16. That's me! How shall I be at the end of this year? Sweet and fresh and naïve yet or changed? *Qui sabit?* A year is a long time. But 16 sounds like a lovely age.

Wish me luck.

Fortuna ad Joana Brietta sexdecem. Evermore and evermore. Amen.

Good Night. Happy birthday to me!

Woden's Day, Wednesday, December 21, 1938

First day of winter—Woden's mystic day. I got a Christmas card today from "Wotan of Walhalla," but I suspect Daddy. Us and our jokes.

P.S. Girls at church all very interested about George Rossit driving me home. I had no idea. We went into Walgreens after choir practice and spent [an] hour in [the] red leather room. Much fun.

Christmas Day, Sunday, December 25, 1938

Well, the ancient Yuletide customs—pagan and traditional—come their sweet way again. Christmas at 16 is something one has only once, and I am feeling very secret and mysterious. You must honor me. . . .

Yesterday night Mom and I went to the midnight service at St. Peter's. Strange how the old things pass. . . . I think being the Virgin last Sunday made me feel more personal about Christmas. The Babe seemed a bit more real and the stars are bright points in the sky. Always, always, though, I can feel my arms beating up against emotion—superstition fighting to understand and break through the chrysalis. Joseph (he who was Joseph and called me Mary) was sitting on the other side of church from us. After communion he and the man with him got up and moved across from us. We looked when the other did not look.

Pagan holly and evergreen covered the church.

Today I went to 11:00 service to sing. Still the butterfly fighting to free itself . . . Santa left a letter and his portrait in my stocking but his writing was like Mom's.

Also got: blue housecoat, teal blue dress, black suede pumps, two slips, pajamas.

Woden's Day, Wednesday, December 28, 1938
I have been sleeping since Christmas but now I must settle down and read *The Iliad* in earnest—also Latin—ugh. And yet they say "Oh carefree youth"—esp. *The Iliad*—three times I've been supposed to read it and each time I've escaped but no more. Fate is vengeful. She's catching up on me.

Hello!

No faeries today yet....

I fear me for their existance...

Well — we must be brave...

—

Went downtown shopping tot

Afterwards sat near G N St Stist

by the Fountain of the Fates an

redd Robinson's Tristrans ...

.... such a moonlight on w

rills, feeling it gives one ...

Sat on the little stone to the

if the found while the pigeons

rose and drifted, fluttering a

me — Fat-necked curious fello

with red feet and peady ey

surrounding me, hopeful of pe

And if I moved a foot or tu

a page — they rose in clouds

beating the air hecticly — fle

only to drift down again an

watch with their heads cocke

while I read.......

..... maybe they were in

1939

"Gee, growing up is painful."

Wednesday, January 4, 1939

Well, today life went on. We're starting metabolism in Bio Sci—two classes of people believing in:

Vitalism—that life is something beyond a combination of matter and energy.

Mechanism—that life can be explained by a knowledge of matter and energy.

I don't know, but I rather think I believe in vitalism, despite the much-publicized disillusion of Modern Youth. Oh well. . . . Today is a misted fogged day, all the dreams floating around under the white rayed street lamps. . . .

In Humanities today I asked, "Achilles* was the one with the heel?" and everyone roared and roared.

---

*The Greek hero whose only vulnerable spot was his heel.

P.S. Patty says George Hodge told her she and I were the most popular girls here. Hmm. And we solemnly agree.

Saturday, January 7, 1939

Measured myself at Girls Club yesterday: bust: 32; hips 33½; waist about 26; height 5 ft. 1½ inches; weight is 101½.

Monday, January 9, 1939

One person said I looked like Anne Shirley and another that I looked like Andrea Leeds all today. Hm—it used to be Miriam Hopkins.* Oh well. Good Night. I travel to the Hittite Empire. . . .

Sunday, January 15, 1939

Hello! Well today was Sunday. We've been studying atoms and molecules, energy and matter in Bio Sci. Today in church I heard them talking about the "resurrection of the dead"—the "world without end"—and such things and all the sudden I thought of the Conservation of Matter. All the other things seem to mean (being interpreted) only that: the Conservation of Matter—what a prosaic phrase for a philosophy. Nothing is ever lost—ever created or begun—ever dead and ended.

That means all matter goes on forever. When I die, perhaps I shall lie in the cool earth, and grass and flowers and weeds will send their roots to find food in me—in my dead body—perhaps then useless to me. But useful to the flower root—the thin, sensitive white root hairs shall enter me and use me. And the flowers will grow. And a deer will eat the

_____

*All popular actresses in the 1930s.

92

flower and a man will shoot the deer and his family eat the deer and I, I shall be in them all. And who shall know me then? Will all my secret atoms ever find their way together again to form the same cohesion that made me? Such is the conservation of matter and shall my soul too find a use? Or ever cling together with my original atoms again?—In the church I looked at the wood—the hard, varnished wood of the pew and I thought, "This was once springy wood through which the sap of life went up in spring." Oh, is nothing ever lost? It gives you a secret everlasting feeling to know part of you at least will never be lost.

[Went] to Art Institute to look at Modern Art. On way out, met Bruce Collins who gave me that "I didn't expect to see *you* here" look and exchanged repartee:

Me: "Hello—improving your mind?" (Brightly—it needs it).

He: "Oh no" (not that!), "waiting for someone . . ."

Monday, January 16, 1939

In art today we were talking about Greek temples and the parts, one of which is the "necking,"* and Miss Lee says innocently, "After necking, what?" And the class howled and Bruce said sweetly, "The cornice," but I wonder.

Wednesday, January 18, 1939

Well—made deadline in *Midway* office by writing till 6:10. I am promoted on masthead to "feature writer." Very newspapery atmosphere there—typewriter pounding, scribbling of pencils, people running in and out with hats on—and much yelling, "How many words did you want?" Also competitive

---

*"Necking" is an architectural term for part of the capital of a column.

noises from the next-door *Correlator*[*] office through skylight. Oh—such is the life *vita dulcis*.[†]

Monday, January 23, 1939

Hello! Well, life goeth ever on, even if I do feel rotten. However, I do not feel rotten. I still believe in the conservation of matter which is pretty consistent in me. Almost two weeks now. Last Friday in Humanities we were talking about Greek religion versus ours. And, oh, our atheistic class! One boy—John Newmark—wanted to take a vote of how many people actually believed in heaven and hell. The class was so incredulous that the teacher refused the ballot. She is so naïve and yet not. But she has almost succeeded in making me hate Humanities [for] which I will not forgive her—Miss Campbell.

After class, Frazier came up to me and walked down hall *mecum*[‡] and says he:

He: "Do you believe in heaven and hell, Joan?"

I (overcome by conservation of matter): "No, I'm afraid I don't. I suppose that disagrees with you?"

He: "No, it doesn't. That's good. I don't either. What do you believe in?"

Me: "Oh, I don't know—conservation of matter right now. It's awfully compelling."

He: "Yes, it is. I guess I believe in that, too. But doesn't that disprove immortality?"

I: "Oh, I don't know. It means we'll live again in flowers, doesn't it?"

---

[*]The school yearbook.
[†]Latin for "sweet life."
[‡]Latin for "with me."

He: "Yes . . . Mr. Mayfield (Bio Sci teacher) makes it all so personal, doesn't he? You know—I wanted to be cremated."

I: "Oh, do you? I used to want to, too, but now it seems as though I'd be cheating the Earth, you know."

He: "Yes, I know."

I: "I did want to be cremated, but now I feel a sort of duty toward the Earth. . . . Of course it seems awful to rot away in the . . ."

He: "Yes . . . but I suppose . . . I saw a cremation once!"

Me: "Oh—what was it like?" (I wanted to asked how it smelled, but he thinks I'm crude as it is.)

He: "Oh, it was behind a glass wall and it shriveled up and . . ."

I: "Oh—Oh!" (thinking rotting in the cool sweet earth is more natural)

He: "And then . . ." etc., etc.

And so we reached the locker room and I staggered to Modern Dance.

Speaking of Modern Dance, we've got a new exercise now. I'll try to sketch it if you promise not to laugh—it's sort of a contract and expand thing:

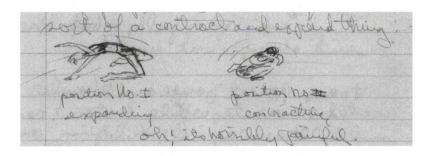

Oh, it's horribly painful. And then there's this:

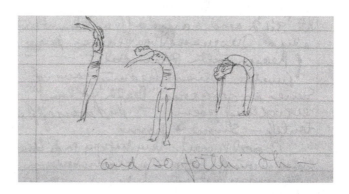

And then one more—falling to floor in [three] counts:

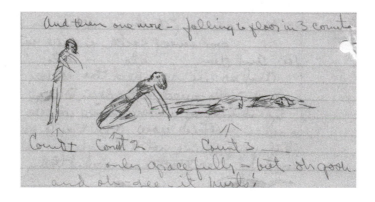

Only gracefully—but oh gosh and oh—gee—it hurts!

Wednesday, January 25, 1939

Hi ya! Well, the *dulcis vita* goeth on. Ever goeth on . . .

The championship fight has just been fought and Louis beat Lewis in 29 seconds.* Truly the Age of Speed. The

---

*Joe Louis beat John Henry Lewis in a boxing match.

announcer on the radio had a hard time saying Joe and John Henry. The pugilists of today are the gladiators of yesterday and the what (?) of tomorrow: Oh well . . .

After school went to *Midway* office to make deadline. My "Aunt Polly" advice column this week. One kid writes, "*The Iliad* makes me ill. *The Odyssey* makes me odd and Homer makes me homely. What shall I do?" And thus and so . . .

Ollie and I were talking. He complains that he is but a lowly sports writer. Then we shook hands on something and says he, "Gosh, how small your hands are!"

And I says: "Oh, that comes from biting my fingernails." And then we went into a discussion of fingernail biting.

All the while Hazel was making supposedly sarcastic comments on the progress of Ollie and me. (I had only 53 words—and he only one paragraph. But it had taken us almost an hour.) Finally Dick says, "How's your paragraph coming, Ollie—of course, I realize that you've got pleasant company there, but—" And Ollie blushed and I ignored and we both scribbled furiously.

Thursday, January 26, 1939

Vera's father is dead. Gee, I came home and Mom told me. I used to play cards with him and tell jokes and I saw him last Saturday and today he is dead . . . and the Spanish War is over and the Chinese War is going on and 8,000 people died in the Chile Earthquake and people all over the world are eating their suppers and doing their homework (as I shall) and laughing and reading and moving about in lighted rooms and a man I know is dead.

It's funny . . . coming home on the L tonight I made an equation—a geometric equation to prove that Life cannot be canceled.

Matter + Energy + X = Life

Matter and Energy cannot be canceled.

Therefore: you cannot cancel Life.

But I don't know. I will not be speaking to Mr. Love any more.

I feel low to be eating and writing in here and doing my homework when someone is dead . . . but someone is always dead. [Eight thousand] people that other people knew are dead in Chile and I speak thus.

Barcelona fell to the Rebels and a war is over and I talk thus—

Good Night.

Saturday, January 28, 1939

Vera's father, Mr. Love, was buried today, and Ruth Billman and I went to the funeral. He was at the Chapel on Clark St., and I thought he looked very still there, [he] who was so nimble in life. We sat there and the streetcars rumbled and he lay very white and the man said things that had little meaning. . . . It's odd he died a year and a few hours exactly from the time I first saw him. Vera and I were going to the Senior Drama and I called for her and she introduced me to her father and Harry and her mother. We waited while she got ready, at first in silence and then I sat on a chair and it creaked and creaked. They had been playing pinochle. That was January 24, 1938. He will not play pinochle anymore. . . .

It's funny, but as we sat there all the funny little inconsequential things kept passing into my mind: the time I went there with my new shoes and he properly admired them and we listened to Olsen and Johnson* on the radio. That was

*Vaudeville comedians.

last summer, early in June. . . . All the times we all played pinochle together and would listen to the *Green Hornet* or *The Count of Monte Cristo*. . . . The time we went to see Vera dance and he looked so young and amiable in his unstylish cap. . . . The night it rained and I waited for it to stop at their house with him and Mrs. Love and we looked up *rain* and *storm* and *tornado* and *cyclone* in their fancy encyclopedia and *tornado* said "see cyclone," and *cyclone* said "see tornado." And they started to reminisce about their youth in Iowa—how he slept out in the rain with some other boys and about the old swimming hole and Mrs. Love told how at first they didn't know whether he was going to marry her or her sister. . . .

That was very long ago and he is married to the dark Earth now. And he has begotten children and passed from life and—oh poor Mrs. Love! She won't laugh about that Iowa youth now. He will not play pinochle or listen to the "Lone Ranger" anymore. . . . All this I thought sitting in there while the man read words without meaning and the Conservation of Matter did not seem to satisfy me. It failed me then. . . . He looked very still and peaceful but I who was longing for death no longer desire it. Oh poor, poor Mrs. Love! As I sat there, I looked about and there in the front row I saw Billy and I thought: he too will be dead and he may grow up and have children and suffer or laugh much but he shall surely die. Everyone in this room shall surely die. And I saw Vera, and Harry, who will too die, looking serious and holding his mother. Oh, poor Mrs. Love . . . I remember the time Mr. Love kissed her when he came home from work. . . .

It was very still in there. I did not cry at first, but, when I saw him just before they put the cover on, I thought: "He will never see the light again," somehow the conservation of matter slipped away and I began to cry because he would never see the light again. . . . It was snowing out, a wet, melting snow, and the sky was grey and colorless. . . .

Andy took Ruth and me out to the cemetery in his car. He had on a sailor suit and we talked of the navy and dancing and the weather and somehow he was dead in front of us. We got out there and the pink and purple flowers looked strange on the thin white snow—the new snow melting on the petals. It was covered with a blanket of flowers and they lowered it with meaningless words. I looked at the flowers and thought he will not see color again. . . . It was all over, we turned and walked slowly away and my feet dragged through the snow. All the time the man had been talking, you could hear the snow falling. . . .

I saw Harry and his eyes were strained and red. He's wearing glasses now, too much reading, I suppose. I shall have the same fate, heaven forbid. But he and I and we all shall have the same final fate and heaven shall not forbid. . . . I saw Mr. Love last Saturday a week ago today in a darkened room, and as I went he said, "Good-bye, Joan." I had not known he meant it. And now the cold wet snow is falling on the broken Earth. . . . Oh poor Mrs. Love!

Here I have been writing when there is nothing to write, because there is nothing to write about death. As I sat in the room, I thought this is the most ancient thing here and not one of us can say a thing about it. And there is nothing to say.

Mr. Love will not play pinochle or try out my Modern Dance with me or us any more. . . . Remember when he tried the newest exercise I could not do. It was very hard but he was nimble. His limbs are not nimble now and the Conservation of Matter is not so sweet to me. . . .

Monday, January 30, 1939

Ate in living room tonite, and we pretended it was the Palmer House [Hotel] (steak and mushrooms) and Daddy was ape-man—much fun.

Hope wintry wind blows, blows tomorrow, so I won't have to go to school. Think of all the unemployed people getting jobs shoveling snow now—(How noble of me!)—and how it ought to snow.

"Hear me, Zeus!"

'Cause I haven't done today's Latin yet and in another day could maybe catch up on homework. Oh well . . .

Snow is deep and looks like the snow on the mountains of an unknown land. The kids are building snow houses (igloos) and snow forts.

Mr. Love has a warm blanket now above him. I'm glad the snow is clean and fluffy—

Good Night!

I started to think how funny it would be if I would die now and traced "Joan Wehlen 1939" on the steamed window.

When I grow up, I'm going (maybe) to *Daily News* and say (as of the book on jobs I read):

"You lack human interest. What you need is an Inquiring Reporter and I'm it. I offer free services for a week. Whoopee—"

And then I shall walk off with the job!!

Wednesday, February 1, 1939

Oliver was in office again and tried to help me make up "Aunt Polly" answers and, in disgust at one of my lower puns, said, "Oh, why did I ever become affiliated with you?"

Me (not knowing what "affiliated" means—having only heard it in reference to gas and coal, you know: Affiliated Gas and Coal Works): "Oh!"

Met fellow on L today who said yesterday, "Gee, I wish I were back in school again," for my benefit. He stared unbelievingly and I calmly read the Beech-Nut gum ad. . . .

Man with derby and politician air next to me on way home after observing me struggling with Cicero suddenly said, "Here, would you like this paper," and offered it to me, apparently thinking I was reading Latin too painfully.

I said, "Oh, no thank you."

He: "I can't read it, see, without my glasses."

Me: "Oh—" (and fainted into Cicero).

Thursday, February 2, 1939

Saw paramecium dying today. It went slower . . . and slower (after darting around so blithely!) and finally stopped. And I wept bitterly—and inwardly. Boo hoo. What happened to all his live protoplasm . . . and who can answer that?

Sunday, February 5, 1939

Church this morning. Did I tell you I've been wearing my hair page boy? Today I didn't however—wore it pretty and fluffed over my face, and with my green knitted hat I looked sorta cute.

Of course I wear rouge nowadays and a horrid but glamorous orangey lipstick that matches the yarn flowers on my brown sweater.

Took communion today but my conscience bothered me—I'm not sure what I think nowadays and there's no use being hypocritical. (Anyhow, I was hungry.)

Friday I had a horrid *Iliad* test. A "well-greaved man" is one with good leg armor as I discovered (and rightly!) by the process of elimination. They hadn't invented chain mail then, had they?

Jim Alter had been ribbing Barbara, the other third page editor, for using both "Aunt Polly" and "Inquiring Reporter" on the page for her week (space fillers). So I just laughed and laughed on Friday because, next week being his page:

He: "Oh Joan—wait a minute!" Comes up to me and begins to walk up hall with me, muttering incoherently.

Me (brightly): "Yes?"

He: "Gurgle, gurgle." We finally reached girls' locker room and I waited for him to speak. Finally: "Could you have both 'Aunt Polly' and 'Inquiring Reporter' columns next week?"

Me: "Oh—oh, yes, of course—" (smirk, smirk).

He (dashing away): "Gurgle!"*

Gee, growing up is painful. Half the time, I don't know what to do with my legs; they always feel like stret-stretching away. Maybe I'm growing. And it's the strangest age: I feel grown upper than before, but not quite. I'm not quite so filled with old wonders but I keep finding new ones. I question all laws—am unpatriotic and atheistic to common standards. I get mad at flag-wavers and over religious people. Look quite grown up and walk along soberly enough but when no one is looking, I skip and slide on the ice. Well, I suppose the lovely

---

*The 1940 yearbook, *The Correlator*, comments, "Feature editor Joan Wehlen suffered most, for there was seldom enough space for her excellent material."

age will all be over someday, but I am holding it fast; I have found beauty in color and line and life and the shadows our little red lamp makes on Mephistopheles (our plant so called because it looks like the devil!). I shall not forget life even if I lose it. It is a lovely world: the sky is blue and the snow is melting and I can hear the Earth expanding. Spring only comes once when you're 16. I must keep my eyes open for it or I shall miss it in the rush (could I, at 16?), well—"Shades of night are falling fast."*

Wednesday, February 8, 1939

Mom looking at my science homework about reproduction now and every once in a while she shakes her head numbly; she's just said, "When I fell in love with Daddy, I never thought it would come to this!" Oh well . . .

Sunday, February 12, 1939

Went to Buckingham Theatre yesterday to see *Blondie* and that rip-roaring melodramatic serial *Mark of the Wilderness*. (Time off: Marian Anderson's singing "Comin' Thro' the Rye" on the radio now—10:20 or so). Fellow there followed me up the aisle and started to talk to me but I chewed popcorn nonchalantly. . . .

I walked home past the old places where Betty and I used to walk—and Shirley. Where we met Jimmy Frankel and Stanley and told them the great secret: "The Jolies Amies are going to give a play, but don't tell anyone." We knew how to get publicity. And they danced around us as we went to the Century [Cinema]. The time Beth, Shirley and I were initiated into that club of Shirley Powell, Denise

*A line from Longfellow's "Excelsior."

104

and Jimmy, etc. And we were brought blindfolded into that great snowbound field on Wellington. And Jimmy took my hand and led me up and down the special paths that we had to go on to be among the initiate. Gee, how time passes. Remember when Betty and Shirley and I used to play college girl or business girl up in Betty's attic—oh, the fun we had. And now Shirley in Detroit and Betty at Lake View and I at U-High. Oh well . . .

"Time, oh, time, in your fleeting way." There is no way to stop it. The years go on. And these too are good. . . . Good Night!

P.S. Remember the time Betty and I passed the boy and girl in the park kissing in the middle of [the] block as though they would never see each other again? And Betty and I gaped like the crude barbarians we were?

Tuesday, February 14, 1939

Well—St. Valentine's Day is here! Whoops Whoops! This year I guess we're all too old, or else progressive education has stopped our sentiment, so we gave out no Valentines. And I didn't receive any lace colored red hearts as of yore. Remember the comic Valentine I got from Burton way back in seventh grade? And then Shirley and Betty and I would go over to Shirley's house and play Valentine store with handsome young man, sweet salesgirl and then series of comic characters—huffy old lady—lovesick boy—stage struck female—shy sweetheart—bold young man—brusk but lovable businessman and so forth. O they were the days! What imagination kids have—and what character playwrights we would have been! We discussed the cast for *Gone with the Wind* today.

Thursday, February 16, 1939

Well—what've we got that the Greeks didn't have? All the sad day I thought that as I was reading in Humanities yesterday. I looked around the room and everyone was reading and outside the snow was falling—and what have we that the Greeks didn't have? They knew about evolution—or some semblance of it—they knew about eclipses and so forth—and oh—their poetry! Oh, the wonderful, wonderful Greeks!

Rode home yesterday on L with Milton—he's a socialist or communist or something. Oh my!

Rode home again with Milton, also with Dick—they argued about politics and I watched the snow. . . .

Must do Cicero, Fourth Orations Part II—

Good Night! Love—!

Saturday, February 18, 1939

I saw *Idiot's Delight** downtown today—oh when the next war comes, and it will come, let me remember that everyone is in the closed room of his own body and thought, for all the mad noise and shouting. The peace speech in the movies that says when the war comes,

> "Love will be turned to hatred,
> Courage to terror
> And hope to despair."

There is something final about the movie—and when Irene says, "Perhaps we two cheap people with our two cheap lives are the only real people in the whole world." That sense of being the only really existent [thing] comes to everyone, I suppose, at times.

---

*An antiwar film with Clark Gable and Norma Shearer.

And the peace-preacher is killed, the little Herr Doktor waddles off with his rats, from saving the human race to aid in killing it—the young Englishman goes to smear the earth with his lifeblood, and the amiable little peasant goes out in his ridiculous uniform to a war he cannot win in. But Harry and Irene shout when the bombs are loudest and play the piano madly when the after-quiet of the attack is come. That is the war that will come to *my* generation. We are no different: every generation has been burdened with a war. It is just that this is *my* generation.

Evelyn and I are to start teaching at Erie Chapel* next week. Saturday morning. Came away from there and man came up and said, "Can you give an ex-serviceman a little carfare." I gave him a dime. Police car came up—asked questions. Was going to get back my dime as he had just gone into a saloon, said the policemen. I said, "Never mind," and Evelyn and I went on, only a little disillusioned, but moaning loudly about my lost faith in human nature—on home. Then to *Idiot's Delight.* . . .

After *Idiot's Delight*, I walked out of the show and down the broad night streets of the Loop. Up State—past Field's—Carsons—Palmer House—people passed—but all seemed to be going in the opposite direction. It was very quiet and I could not hear myself walk. The earth was melting, the wind stirred my hair and blew my coat back—I had on flat-heeled shoes and the act of walking was restful—the lights flashed on and off—the spring wind lay in the tall buildings and the shadows fell on the streets as on a well-staged movie set. . . . Everything was set, but nothing happened. But *someday* it will

*At 1347 West Erie Street; this "neighborhood house" helped immigrants and aided WPA workers.

and the quiet street will be a mass of broken bricks and fallen columns. And perhaps the lights will still flash on the empty street. Then I walked down the street and thought: "Everyone I am passing will surely die and color, light and life shall lie within the secret earth."

And the thought that people I knew too may die—even though I know them—and I walked on—and got into a bus and the woman in front of me smoked and the man behind talked business and we passed the white lights of the river, "And white of river light too shall dim that glimmers on the shore."

Well, that was about enough—home—now to bed. [Nineteen forty] is next year. Good Night!

Wednesday, February 22, 1939

Hello again! This is me. I went to choir for tonight and the thin baby moon was sleeping wide-eyed over the western house-tops. We sang the Magnificat* and somehow since the Christmas pageant, I know why Mary said it—I thought I knew. . . . Nick Wolf walked me home and he tried to guess who I liked but I was quite secretive. Father Willis talked tonight—who works among the mentally sick of Chicago. He smiled at me after service (pitter pat!) quite nicely and so did the nice man in choir who was slightly inebriated last Friday night. Hank looked so winsome playing the organ in his *very* churchly clothes with his hair falling on his forehead.

The church was dark and, as Father Willis talked, I got the idea he was speaking to an empty church. The night was

---

*From the Gospel of Luke, a book of the Bible. It is the response Mary makes to her cousin Elizabeth when she tells her that she is to bear Jesus.

very dark with shivering stars and the baby moon trembling in the cold. The pillars of the church are of the Corinthian order (just showing off my Greek art!). Well, after church we were going to get a Coke, but no one had a nickel.

Good Night!

Thursday, February 23, 1939

Everyone's talking about "Aunt Polly" column. Heard two girls in gym today discussing it. Says one: "Gee, but that column's cute—the answers are so funny. I wonder who writes it?" Other girl: "I don't know—maybe Annette Weiss." I was going to continue eavesdropping blithely, but Ruth Cooper gave me away as to what I was to much laughter. By the way, did I tell you? When I went into the doctor's office for an admit on Monday—half the school seemed to be there. I waited long hours between Ned Rorem and Caroline Wheeler. Suddenly, Frazier shouts, "Oh, Aunt Polly!"

Me: "Sh-sh!" (Finger to mouth!)

Jim Trow: "That's right—keep it quiet. We've got enough epidemics going around as it is. . . . Are you Aunt Polly?"

Me: "Yes . . . do I look like an epidemic?"

And so on while all the other people watched.

Wednesday, March 1, 1939

Today was the *Midway* deadline and as *Midway* office was crowded, Frazier and Bruce invited me into the French room where Bruce was editing "Potpourri"—so I went to write and bite my pencil and Rosalind Wright came along to chaperone or something. They three talked French while I scribbled or tried to—finally Rosie left and I continued; they started to talk about my hat in French as I gathered from "Joan's *chapeau*" or something of the sort. They said it was "*de trop*" and so forth which unfortunately I could translate—of course it was a little screwy.

Finally we got put out of French room—wandered into art room and studied modern results of p.e. (progressive education), limbs floating around, etc. Oh well—Bruce draped himself up as some Roman in a green tablecloth affair and we all howled heartily till we saw the cleaning man was spying on us. Then Frazier and I began to discuss the Second Oration (our outside reading) which is decidedly *not* a subject for mixed company.*

Midway office was still crowded so I retreated in *Correlator* office where Kenneth was typing. He has a unique method of bouncing paper off typewriters but I won't go into that. I swore I'd be quiet as a mouse and started out to do so. Frazier and Bruce came in—talked to me—I tried to be quiet but no can do. Frazier began to recite his Greek something or other and Kenny shouted vainly, "Quiet!" Then Bruce finally retreated and Oliver came in to write his sports page—got along O.K. for a while, then Dick came in and tried to figure out his pet ambition which was the "Inquiring Reporter" question this week. Then we started to talk about the assembly today and

---

*Presumably because of its references to lust, atrocities, and rape.

he wouldn't let me answer anyone else, which got Oliver mad and delighted Kenny.

Says Dick: "Listen, I'm speaking to Joan. Please be quiet."

Oliver: Glare, glare.

Kenny: "Ha-Ha!"

Me: Gulp, gulp.

And so on . . .

Then we started on ambitions again (Kenny had given up by this time) and no one could think of anymore till Kenny said, "To seduce Mae West," which nice little girls didn't talk about when I was young, so I gulped and continued to smile brightly and changed the subject (more or less).

Finally Kenny put us out, as he was going home. I turned in my article and Dick lugged in my coat from the deserted *Correlator* office. He put it on me too and as it was the horrid seventh grade relic (as my other's at the cleaner's) all the holes showed gorgeously. Oh well . . . someday I'll be a genius. Bruce wants to be a psychiatrist (I can't even spell it!) but I wouldn't let him examine my brain though Frazier said I wouldn't miss it. (Grrrr.) Oh well—on with life—Humanities today also *Antigone* in RWC*—very tragic—fellow marries mother—and Mr. Denton couldn't understand how his daughter would be his half-sister then—which the class undertook to explain to Mr. Denton—oh well—

Latin as always.

I got highest marks in test on Second Oration and third in sight reading test. Not so bad—

Good Night and Good Night!!!

*Readings in Western Civilization.

Sunday, March 12, 1939

Little boy started to walk down Broadway with me this morning. He gravely regarded me all the way, never saying a word, and when I turned down Cornelia, he came back and turned too. Always gravely regarding me. I thought, "He's pretty young for a pick-up" (he must have been about nine) but, on later consideration, I have concluded he thought I was a foreign spy and was tracking me to Fu Manchu—I don't know. Anyhow he quit after a while and went into a house on Cornelia—never saying a word. I waved good-bye cheerfully at him and he seemed to think me mad. . . .

Monday, March 13, 1939

Barbara and I stopt at dime store. Weighed ourselves and Barbara looked at paper dolls while I tried to get ball in hole at toy counter. No could do. Little boy standing beside me said disgustedly, "Can't you do that?"

Me: "No."

He: "Let me."

He couldn't do it either.

Home on streetcar. Woman saw my Cicero, smiled sympathetically, then started to discuss him. She was pretty, dark-haired and not so old. When we parted, she said, "Don't work too hard on that," and I said, "I'll try to control myself." There are nice people—lots of them—the round world over and I feel fine—

Sunday, March 19, 1939

This morning Carol and I discovered the room upstairs in church. It was this way: we were trying out a new dance step—"one, two, three, kick"—on the second landing and only just stopped as Father Carr came along. So we went into the room. It had a mediaevil [*sic*] look: deep windows with many paned glass . . . deep carpeted, fireplace, sunlight on [the] street beyond and deep sofas in [the] room. Carol began to play the piano and I went to fetch our things from the landing windowsill. Ran plump into last year's Joseph and fled with a breathless, "Oh!" He must have thought something wrong. In the room again: Carol played "Ave Maria," "Humoresque," etc., while I wandered about room looking at old pictures. Then I sat at one of the deep stoned windows and opened it and the spring air moved my hair. Outside people were passing, going to church—moving dreamily in the spring sunlight.

"Life is a loom, weaving illusions."[*]

I sat there at peace on the arm of a chair, watching. That is what I am by nature anyway—a watcher. The old yellow grass was on the ground but there was a hint of new green, too. The sky was blue with flecks of whipped-cream-white clouds. The red bricks of [the] building across the street were beautiful, as was the torn kite caught in the bare treetops, early leafed. Carol was playing "God Bless America" and I thought such a scene might appear anywhere in the world— red brick on a sunlit street in Germany, people moving, in England, Austria, Russia . . . anywhere but here. I saw the red brick, physically beautiful, and the people passing in a "Träumerei."[†] The noises from the street drifted in and as Carol played, I made the sign of the cross, I blessed the world "for that I loved."

---

[*]From Vachel Lindsay's poem "The Chinese Nightingale: A Song In Chinese Tapestries." The original has "illusion" in the singular.
[†]"Daydream" or "reverie"; a piece of piano music by Robert Schumann.

I felt I had the right to bless, feeling blessed—seeing the dream of life. "I bless ye, for that I love." And slowly the time passed and Carol played on . . . and time came for us to go. And we went. And were holier for the quiet few minutes I am sure than for the restless hour in church.

I was wondering: if Jesus lived, did he have the same desires and wants we have and, if he did, was he right not to yield to them, and if he did not, was he perfect man? I'm not being blasphemous, but I think it's wrong to believe a thing till your mind has examined it, etc. Well . . . Good Night.

P.S. Hitler has just taken all of Czechoslovakia. But is Germany wrong? When in school, I made a pity-  ing remark for the Germans. Doris Westfal said, "Well, I don't care very much what happens to them." Oh, I think that's so wrong! What else could Germany have had after the war except that a dictator would spring up—if not Hitler, another.

We must be tolerant and never hypocritical. Well, if there is another war, may we—oh, why say end war—we know we will not. . . . And next year is 1940—well . . . Good Night.

P.S. The Ides of March is passed and I had not noted it—a sure sign of old age. . . .

Sunday, March 26, 1939

Went with Florence Sargis to see *What a Life**—very good. High school life as it is. . . . Ha ha. . . . Met at the Institute and saw the engraving exhibit there. An O.K. evening—went to St. Chrysostom's for counselors' meeting.

He introduces me as "Miss Wehlen who knows all about birds, stars, trees, flowers, *reptiles* and *insects*." Well, and then later on says he: "Miss Wehlen, I'll bet not half these people know the difference between Norway pine and white pine."

Me (never having heard of either): "I'll bet they don't."

He: "Those who think they know raise their hands. Now, don't you see, Miss Wehlen?" (which I had no intention of doing. Some kid gives half-baked difference better than I could do). And then says He: "Well, he hasn't got the real reason, has he?"

Me (bravely): "No."

He: "Shall we tell them?"

Me: "Gulp!"

He: "Well, the Norway pine has two needles to a bunch and the white has five and the Norways are about 1½ to 2 inches long. Isn't that right?"

Me: "About 1½ inches." (Never having heard of it but being defiant.)

He: "And it has a sort of pinkish cast to the bark."

Me: "Oh, would you say that?"

He: "I mean the Norway pine."

And we all died happily—help—help!!!!!

---

*A 1939 film with Jackie Cooper.

Tuesday, April 4, 1939

All in Bi Sci who had Latin leanings and *all* in Latin were much amused by my logical dissertation on frog's brain in recent test. We had to name three parts of the brain. As I knew the back part was cerebellum, I concluded the front part must be antebellum which I solemnly put on my paper. Mr. Mayfield handed it back today with the sole noncommittal remark, "Means 'after the war.'" Oh well—Life goeth on.

P.S. Kelly has won, the man on radio has just said, though vote counting is not completed.[*]

Saturday, April 8, 1939

Hello. It's almost Easter day, 1939, now and somehow it sounds like a momentous date. Italy has invaded Albania and King Zog and Geraldine (who's half American) and their three-day old son have fled to Greece. The Albanians are fighting, but it's a losing battle and bombs are dropping in the rugged quiet creamy country of the past. Triana has fallen. . . .

"Peace I leave with you, my peace I give unto you."[†]

Easter Day is coming 1939 and I feel sure it will all begin now. What, I'm not sure, but the end and the beginning are come. . . .

It's past midnight now . . . Easter Day. "I am the Resurrection and the Life: He that believeth in me, though he were dead, yet shall he live."[‡]

---

[*]Edward J. Kelly, Democrat, winning his third of four terms in office as mayor of Chicago.
[†]From John 14:27.
[‡]From John 11:25, spoken by Jesus Christ. According to Christian belief, Easter is the day of Christ's resurrection.

In one of the sermons yesterday, Father Carr said that those who look back on the prewar days—pre the last war—1910–11, 1912–1913—seem to be looking back, remembering a dream, so quiet, so peaceful were those days: contrast our present hectic days. I wonder if we shall ever look back on these days as on a dream, and remember them for peace. I wonder if the present is always hectic. . . .

There is not much one can say on Good Friday. . . . Not much on Easter, but on this time before morning there is nothing at all to say.

Easter Day, April 9, 1939

Hi! Well, I went to 11:00 service [in church] with George Hodge this morning. Actually was on time. Wore my new tweed swagger coat and powder blue hat.

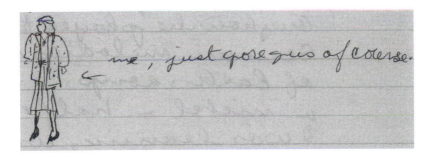

me, just gorgeous of coarse.

This afternoon spent at home, Mom and I in our separate cells. I was lucky, I had the living room with the radio. Heard "Träumerai." Such haunting music, but I can't even hum the tune now.

Well, it seems my prophecy about Easter 1939 is wrong but perhaps the world is to go to pieces today. Well, "Peace on Earth, good will to men."

Father Carr in his sermon lambasted Hitler and Mussolini. It's easy to accuse them now, but he wouldn't accuse the greedy statesmen who laid the foundations for the next war at Versailles.

Sunday, April 16, 1939

Today went to church. Afterwards George Hodge asked to walk me home. He also had called for me this morning and asked to call for me tonight for Canterbury Guild meeting.

Am going to give up this scribbling as arm is tired for time being.

Man is talking on European affairs on radio. Phooey—F.D.R.'s message may mean peace for the world. Well. "Peace I give unto you, my peace I leave with you—that which the world cannot take away nor steal"—Good Night!

Tuesday, April 18, 1939

Well, no war yet though a major one is predicted within next two weeks by our foreign ambassadors [Joseph] Kennedy and [William Christian] Bullitt.* Pres. Roosevelt's peace plan seems to have died as all such things die. . . . Witness [Woodrow] Wilson, who died disillusioned.

Oh well—

We're done with Cicero at last and his philosophy at the end of the Archias's oration is quite stunning. Nice simple language too—though quite a few subjunctives. All about immortality and whether the soul shall see the name of the man live on into posterity or not. Imagine—Cicero, too,

---

*Bullitt was the first ambassador from the United States to the Soviet Union (1933–1936) and then to France (starting in 1936). Kennedy was the ambassador to Britain.

thought about such things. He must be quite happy now if he can see his name alive today.

Went to card party at church with Eugene Grumbine and Ruth Munro. We had lots of fun. Played rummy and I went into my old habit of saying "cast off" instead of "discard"—just like the old days with Mom and Betty. Remember when we used to call for hemlock? We've been reading about that death of Socrates in school recently. "Virtue is the mean state"—Aristotle—and Socrates was wonderful: "Be of good cheer about death and know this of a truth: that no evil can come to a good man either in life or after death. . . . He and his are not neglected by the gods nor has my own approaching end been by mere chance"—and Betty and I used to call so riotously and joyfully for hemlock. Thus ought it to be.

Then home in the cool drizzle. I rode on Gene's bike and my hat blew off, so I held it and the wind blew through my hair and the tiny raindrops spattered on my face and the breeze was high.

In Humanities no one could think why a "life of sensual enjoyment" was not suitable for our purposes nor who had led a life of contemplation. We're very shy of religion; Miss Campbell says we're the most irreligious class! Two of us admitted going to Sunday school in our class of about 35.

Well—remember me again. Good Night. "Now to Death's brother, sleep."

Wednesday, April 19, 1939

> "God's in his heaven
> All's right with the world."*

---

*From Robert Browning's *Pippa Passes*.

Hi—Whee—life is fine. Got scholarship renewal for next year so do not need to worry about comprehensives—much. Whee!—

Was asked to write the "Skylights" column for the *Midway*—great honor—prize position.

I had my psychology analyzed yesterday. According to that I am "definitely the girl of today with an anticipation of the girl of tomorrow, but when sex rears its ugly head, my morals might be found in *Godey's Lady's Book*,* so straight are they which is perhaps just as well." End quotes. Done in girls' club by Ruth Cooper! Well—Good Night!!!

Monday, April 24, 1939

Walking over to Ida Noyes [Hall] today, I looked up at the golden-bells (forsythia) and caught my breath to see their yellow lace against the bright mid-afternoon sky. I even shyly touched one—to see if it was real.

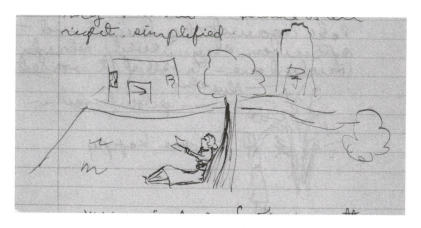

This labeling is the effect of Bi Sci.

---

*A 19th-century woman's magazine.

Speaking of Bi Sci (were we?), Bruce Phemister and I had a long conversation about "Aunt Polly" and so forth over the ovary of a rabbit. I never seem to be able to concentrate over the reproduction of rabbits. . . . Read Terence for first time in class today. Went quite well. I had the second sentence. Hurrah. Terence seems sorta like Shakespeare. Nice hearty plot . . . and certainly much better than Cicero!—Oh my yes! Only eight in the class today but all were convulsed when, on being asked, Cyril solemnly told Miss Macy that there were three parts to the Roman stage: "the front, the middle and the back" (!)—oh well.

Life goeth ever on and on—Hurrah for Alexander—Well—Good Night!

Tuesday, April 25, 1939

[Ruth Cooper] and I met Beryl and Frazier and began to talk—about the Playfest plays among other things. The unspeakable subjects they chose last year. Frazier was telling us some when Mr. Denton passed and really looked quite shocked. I didn't know the subject of one: "sif—."* Oh well, I won't attempt to spell it out but I tried to laugh like the rest of them. Ruth explained on the way home. Oh, oh, no wonder Mr. Denton looked so queer.

Tuesday, May 2, 1939

We are on daylight savings now.

Germany is giving Poland two weeks to give her the Polish corridor. Otherwise war. However, England and France on side of Poland. So Russia too maybe. . . .

---

*Presumably syphilis.

Came home and cooked supper, cleaned up house. Am still alone. Hurt self pushing up heavy [Murphy] bed.* Colon feels busted. Oh well.

Thursday, May 4, 1939

Hello! Whoopee!

I'm feature editor for next year's *Midway*! Hurray, hurray! Gee, I was thrilled, though I sorta suspected it on account of Mary Virginia's mentioning it to me. Oh, well.

Met Father Willis down by the tennis courts this morning and had nice talk. He bowed very courtly to me and I curtseyed in regard to my scholarship. Well—

Home early and sat on stoop doing Terence . . .

Thursday, May 11, 1939

Poor Mom! Our Bi Sci course is too much for her. Tonight I came home talking about the Determination of Sex, etc., all about X and Y chromosomes and all, you know, and well, it was just too much for Mom. Especially since our Bi Sci homework lately has been in "Life and Growth" and "Biography of the Cell." Well, it just overcame Mom. Says she, "I don't think they ought to teach you about all *that*!" Oh well, she's just jealous. But it was funny when *I* started to explain to *her* about sperms and eggs. . . . Don't think me too awful, please, it's just Progressive Education and anyhow, everything's all right if you approach it with a scientific mind (as I told Daddy when *he* started looking at the pictures in our book).

---

*Murphy beds, increasingly popular in the 1920s and 1930s, could be pulled down from inside a closet and put away during the day, thus giving extra room to move about.

Wednesday, May 31, 1939

There was a monkey and organ grinder outside school today and a group of little kids, including me. Bruce Phemister came up, solemnly watched, then, suddenly recognizing me, said, "Oh, I thought you were one of the kids." And I explained to him about me being underfed and we walked on, speaking of Evolution and Ecology (influence of monkey, no doubt).

Friday, June 2, 1939

My two kinds of ancestors have given me too much of everything. I want to believe and be superstitious and there is the cruel harmony in me that beats, "It isn't right, it isn't right." Again and again, the fragile wings of rebellion thud at the deep-founded desire for peace and acceptance.

Monday, June 5, 1939

Well, gee whiz, gosh oh gee!! Whippedy whee! Guess what!!! I won the Pat Diamond Memorial Prize today! My goodness—think of that! It was emblem day, you know, and I just wore my green Nature Study uniform, never thinking of course that I'd be anything and then, as I sat there, all the big shots up in front, you know, Mr. Denton got up and gave his speech and I sat peacefully back and he comes to the part, "This award has been split this first year between—Ruth Thomas a-a-a-a-a-a-and . . . (of course Amy's name just naturally came)—Joan Wehlen." Well, I almost died! You know what I mean: I was surprised! I *was*. Anyhow, I staggered up there, hip-hop—up the huge stage stair and got it. And I do mean $5.00 (five dollars). Oh well.

Tuesday, June 13, 1939

I call ye high heavens and all the little gods to witness that at most I spent this for my comprehensive reviews.

—3½ hours Bi Sci

—1½ hours Humanities

—RWC (but I read the syllabus!)

—½ hour A. P. 1*—read the Constitution

Which is all—so if I get any A's it will be a miracle and a shining example of how not to. That is if I do—oh well, why worry; it's all over now—but the shouting. . . .

[In the middle of Humanities comprehensive], I began to dream over history as I do and all the old thoughts came rushing in, and the sunny Graduate Education room became a 1,000 years old and I am excavator, seeing how little it all meant whether I got an A or an F. Nevertheless, returned to present and concentrated. Oh well . . .

Midway party tonight. I wore my new blue pencil striped silk dress—and got frosting all over it.

Got *Correlator* today—picture of me dissecting frog—or watching it—went to see *Wuthering Heights* tonite with Mom, got home at midnight or later. Good Night!

Thursday, June 22, 1939

Went to *that* place to be examined yesterday. He (Dr. Johnson) gave me a card for the eye place. I've had something in my left eye since I woke up with it Saturday morning. Daddy got me a watch Saturday, too. Elgin,† swell. Went to Mary

---

*The name of this class may have been American Politics.

†A watch company near Chicago.

Joan, age four, with her mother, Neva Wehlen, 1927.

December 938. Joan *center*), age 16, s the Virgin Mary.

THE CHICAGO DAILY NEWS

WEARY LOYALISTS MARCH TO PRISON CAMP

Jan 31-1939

Winding along a road as far as the eye can reach is a weary line of prisoners captured in the Rebel drive on Barcelona and headed for concentration camps. The Loyalist rear guard in Catalonia today was fighting fiercely to impede the Rebels, now along a line undulating westward from the coast, sometimes 20 miles north of Barcelona.

[Associated Press Wirephoto.]

A newspaper clipping that Joan dated January 31, 1939. It shows the defeated loyalists in Spain. Joan wrote at the top, "There is a long story told in the curved line of this picture and a beauty of it."

June 1939. This photo from the U-High *Correlator* yearbook shows a Biological Science frog dissection. Joan stands on the right, wearing a hat.

Joan, age 16, at Camp Oronoko. At the bottom of the photo she wrote, "Trying to look philosophical."

A newspaper clipping from Joan's scrapbook, dated September 5, 1939, depicting British men who were enlisting. Joan wrote, "How many of these will be alive and whole in a year? How many of these blurred faces?"

Joan, age 16, September 1939, holding a newspaper with the headline "Britain Goes to War." She wrote at the bottom, "Melodramatic Moment." That very newspaper is still in her scrapbook; over the headline Joan wrote, "For a moment the world stood still."

Joan, age 16, autumn 1939.

A clipping from the *Chicago Tribune*, December 25, 1939. The caption reads, "Proof that there's no war blackout of freedom in Chicago. Christmas eve on Michigan avenue looking north from Erie street. Cross and beacon on Palmolive building."

MONDAY. DECEMBER 25. 1939.

ll America Alight with Christmas Spirit

Proof that there's no war blackout of freedom in Chicago. Christmas eve on Michigan avenue looking north from Erie street. Cross and beacon on Palmolive building.

NUARY 27. 1940.

dventures After American Vessel Was Captured by Na.

Flint Crewmen Express Their Feelings

Expressing their feelings in a graphic manner, members of the City of Flint crew thumb their noses at the Swastika flag, which the German prize crew flew from the Flint during the period the vessel was in Nazi hands.

A January 27, 1940, newspaper clipping from Joan's scrapbook. In the photo, the Americans thumb their noses at the Swastika. Joan wrote, "Oh humanity! Oh civilization!" She found both sides' dehumanization of the other repugnant.

Some girls are smart and know much,
Some girls are popular, remain as such
But if girls are both, it is true,
That this is something that is new
But JOAN WEHLEN is brilliant you see
And as popular as can be.
For all in school know her so well,
That in our memories she'll always dwell

June 1940. Joan's picture in the U-High *Correlator* yearbook.

Inter-Continent photo

GRAND ADMIRAL RAEDER, Nazi naval commander in chief, greets air pilots.

Surely, even these Germans are human!

A scrapbook clipping, summer 1940. "Surely, even these Germans are human!"

Joan (*right*), age 18, and her chum Betty Crawford in the *Chicago Tribune*, June 1941. Joan's name is misspelled. See Joan's diary entry and drawing from June 8, 1941, of the same event.

Betty Crawford (left) and Joen Wehlen at the concert.

From Joan's school notebooks. These are from the class Methods, Values, and Concepts, which she often mentioned in her diaries. Note, in the middle of the page, the date in French: "onze [11th] decembre 1941." At the bottom is a note in large letters to her friend Betty: "Germany Declared War This Morning!!!"

Joan, age 20, sitting for her engagement photo.

Joan and Bob in 1944 or 1945 at a nightclub. Bob is in his naval uniform.

Stamp's that day and came home and found it. Funny *Daddy* should get *me* a watch for Father's Day. That was Sunday.

I've been reading over the old words I wrote last year this time—I guess that feeling will never come again quite the same, but then neither will any other. . . . Will it? Maybe Eternity is the fourth dimension—another plane from our three but, every once in a while, a moment of our time slips and juts out into Eternity and we get the odd old eternal and unrecapturable feeling. How can I say it? Anyhow, that time is past.

What a nostalgic feeling it is: no matter how long I live or how soon I die, I shall never be 16 in spring again. I'm silly . . . I'm being very strange. Must go to that place about my eye tomorrow. Mustn't think about it.

Remember last spring and Venus glowing in the purple-blue west and me walking home. We can never relive any moment. They're all good, but I'm young.

Why worry! What the hell—Good Night!

Saturday, Midsomer's Day, 1939

Went down to eye place today and he took it out after five hrs' waiting. A big white patch on my eye. Had my picture taken with it . . .

Sunday, June 25, 1939

Nothing is going to change or has ever changed There have been wars and they shall continue to be—like unemployment and slavery and frustrated love and death. Why should we think that just because this is *our* almighty present that now, almost 1940 AD, is the last war—or the first of anything?

Friday, June 30, 1939

Thursday the 28th was *the* dinner-dance. I came horribly late to dinner, but ate the ice cream anyhow. It was at the [Hotel Shoreland] at 55th and the Lake. After dinner we went downstairs where they had chartered a room. It was all decorated up—with red and white balloons everywhere and a slippery waxed floor and pictures of the school and copies of the *Midway* and so forth all over. It was open to Aunt Polly's farewell address—it made me feel almost sad.

I wore my teal blue dress with the pleated skirt—very sheer stockings—my black suede and gold belt and my black suede pumps!!! You should have seen me. And I just had a permanent so my hair was absurdly short and frivolous looking. And I had my little blue net hat sitting over my curls like an idiotic Juliet.

Anyhow, it was just wonderful!! Just wonderful!!! They played a radio and some records and Ollie asked me to dance. Almost all the boys had dark coats with white flannels like in the movies or the magazines. So we danced for a while and then they opened the French doors and Bill Russell asked me to dance with him and we danced out on the veranda. The trees were waving faintly in the night breeze and we could see the moon over them. The lake was dim and shiny and people came out on the fire escape to watch. Some other couples were dancing out there, too, by then. I felt so transferred, so aristocratic, so dream-like—dancing in the night on the veranda of the Hotel Shoreland in Bill Russell's arms . . . just like in the movies. I remember when I was very young, I thought heaven was a beautiful ballroom with women in light dresses dancing with men in evening dress and that I was a little girl watching them through the French doors from the palms outside. That was my idea of heaven, gleaned, I suppose, from an early movie . . . I don't know. Anyhow, I thought of that, dancing outside then—and smiled a little for that little girl, watching from the trees.

And that was my flight at aristocracy. Well . . . it's all over now. . . .

Went downtown yesterday to see *Goodbye, Mr. Chips*—a movie on the book with Robert Donat. Oh, but it was wonderful. I sat there and tears streamed down my cheeks. It was so real—the names—always running through his head.

"Colley, sir."

And when he sat in that schoolroom his wife just dead and the boy read from Caesar, translating jerkily, all the time he was hearing music, music in Vienna . . . music . . . in Vienna. And at the end when he died—all the words that beat into his brain . . .

"Colley, sir."

"Killed in action."

"But I'm 16, and a bit, sir!"

"Hello—o."

"It's the first of April, sir."

"To the future—to the future."

And he sat by the fire and the last words came into his head.

"Good-bye, Mr. Chips."

And the coals glowed brightly.

It was so sad . . . and when he read out the names in the chapel of those killed . . . Max Staefel the gay, warm-hearted German master who died on the other side—his friend . . . and the boys thought and said, "How strange, he was an enemy," and he heard them . . . standing in the snow.

And they read Caesar while the bombs were falling in Brookfield. "This was the kind of fighting in which the Germans busied themselves," and the last blank sight of the plaster on the wall—and all quiet . . .

Oh, it was wonderful. The fellow next to me though got quite familiar—guess it must have been my permanent. He wanted to make sure I enjoyed all the jokes and there I was, bawling. . . .

Monday, July 3, 1939*

Hi—boy am I mad! Boy, could I bop him one—wait'll I tell
you! Wow—grrrr! Well here goes.

Mr. A.† (whom Phyllis and I refer to as my No. 1 because
he is first in the heart of one countryman—), well, he was just
in here, and guess what! Boy, am I mad! I remind him of his
girlfriend! Well—! After all—he even showed me a picture
of her! I shall herewith bop him one! He was in here quite a
while this afternoon and now, 7:40, he's just left again. We
have been discussing: meals, careers, promises, wood ticks—
and (grrr!) his girlfriend. Well—as I said! Well!

Anyhow—stunt night tonight.

Tuesday, July 4, 1939

Night before last went canoe riding with Jimmy—from over
the lake—quite a nice fellow. Moon was like a red heart dripping over the lake and the water was rippleless—like a mirror
she was and the frogs brek-ke-kek-ed‡ and we drifted in close
to the shore—gliding like the night—and the shore was like a
ghost shore—dim—and the trees glowing.

---

*Joan wrote this and the next several entries at Camp Oronoko, where
she was a nature study counselor. Boy campers came the first month,
and girl campers came the second. Some counselors, like Joan, stayed
the entire summer, but many of the male counselors left after the first
month. Joan was the designated nature study counselor for both groups
of attendees. The camp was run by St. Chrysostom's Episcopal Church,
and the parish provided assistance so that poor children could attend.
†"Mr. A." is Joan's nickname for Alex. Over the next few pages, he is
referred to as "he" (and even, on page 131, "my hero").
‡An allusion to *The Frogs* by Aristophanes.

Wednesday, July 12, 1939

Dear Journal—I wish I were writing this as rapturously as I could have Sunday morning but I had no paper then and I'll do my best to recapture the feeling. Anyhow—Saturday night was the barn dance. We went to the barn dance—me in a poke bonnet with rosebuds and blue ribbons. Then afterwards our quartet sang—and then—!!! *He* asked me to go canoe riding with him—oh-oh! It was wonderful. Phyl was going too and there was only one canoe and anyhow we all went together—oh, it was wonderful! We landed at a little beach up the river on the north side and he and I sat in the back and about midnight the gold half-moon rose.

And we talked and talked. And we came to an understanding—about us. Just for the summer. Just for July . . . just for July. He asked me what (being hypothetical) if he kissed me (then I was lying in his arms—because I was cold) and I said I'd blame myself—and that was that. We talked philosophy and life and so forth—oh, he's wonderful! Anyhow, the moon changed from gold to silver and tinged the clouds and I was oh, so cold, though he did his best—and finally Norm, in the front of the boat—called to us on the beach where we had strolled that it was 20 to 2. So we had to go. Some people had built a campfire up the beach and it was still glowing in the distance as we left—with the sand turned to silver dust by the moon—we paddled silently away. Then back and to bed. Phyl and I just too thrilled and life like a black and silver dream! Oh, what a life—bed at 2:30 and then I woke early Sunday morning and lay in bed—feeling good—

Friday, July 14, 1939

Boy, could I bop him one—he said it was soothing to be with me—well—I could tell him a thing or two. Somehow we started humming "Only Make Believe" and the night drifted over and the wind was in the trees. There was a little spring near us and we could hear the water trickling. Well—now it's tomorrow morning—almost 11, and I feel as though I had a hangover—ugh.

P.S. As we parted last night he said he wouldn't ask me out if he didn't like being with me and I said I wouldn't go with him if I didn't like being with him—Aren't we honest?—Ugh!

Saturday, July 15, 1939

Hello!—Here I am, love and lorn and fairly complacent about the whole thing. My hero has gone away to St. Jo for the weekend and I have been drowning my sorrows in work. I mopped and swept our room and dutifully cleaned the spider webs away from the windows—also beautified nature but with aid of Albert Johnson. (Buddy Scott just came in and let a frog loose and he just caught it. Oh well—it's the life!) I smell awful as I just spilled rubber cement all over me trying to fix my shoes. Well—such is life. (I hope he chokes—I keep thinking.)

Am lone and lorn today but am satisfactorily drowning my sorrow (almost) as you see: "This can't be love because I feel so well."*

---

*A Rodgers and Hart song.

Thursday, July 20, 1939

Today *he* had the nerve to come into camp with his girlfriend and some other friends! Boy, was I mad. I was ironing in the kitchen when he came and you should have seen me. I just pretended he was the clothes and did I iron hard—fast and furiously. It was almost funny. I warbled, "Gaily the Troubadour" and cast curses in his direction. Ironing heartily all the while . . .

Friday, July 28, 1939

Oh dear, what can the matter be? Oh dear, what can the matter be? Oh dear! To think all this could happen in one short week! Remember it was just last Thursday I came up from talking to Eddie Adams to make Alex jealous and what did I find myself singing? "Soldier, soldier, won't you marry me?" (He's been at National Guard camp, you know.)

Well, anyhow, he's going away Saturday. Satur-day? That's tomorrow! Oh my gosh!

For the next month I shall be a nun. Ugh! Down the lads! Mrs. B. says to me yesterday, "Well, Joan, I'm sending away all the men you like"—and then she mentioned Eddie and oh, my heart is broken.

Tuesday, August 1, 1939

You know, I have a theory that nothing is wrong if you really want to do it. But I did think and believe—I still do—that to do a thing from inertia or because it's most convenient, unless you really mean it, is wrong. Sometimes it's easy to do a thing—not meaning it—merely carried along and I must remember that, unless I really mean it, I shouldn't do it. Well—keep me straight. Good night!

P.S. That advice machine [at the amusement park in Benton Harbor] said I was a good necker but another one said I was stubborn. I wonder. A third machine said I was a dumbbell. I still wonder.

Thursday, August 3, 1939

He gave me a "To the dearest and sweetest" card and said solemnly, "That's true," and I laughed and gave it to a kid. Oh silly me! And I picked a daisy, white with gold center, and said, "He loves [me], he love me not," on it, and it came out "He loves me not," and he took it from me and said, "That's not true." And I only looked at him and said "How do *you* know," so flippantly. Oh gee—remember. Well, that was only a week ago and am I silly. . . .

What shall I do? Oh dear. I'm really not lovesick. Just enjoying myself and being 16. Anyhow, lovesick isn't the word—silly is closer to it.

Besides, I know he's not good for me. At the very time I want him, I know with my mind I shouldn't. No matter how much he likes me or what we do together, it's nothing new for him. I don't think so anyhow.

Friday, August 4, 1939

Well, this is the morning of Doomsday. Our rivals—the female counselors are already arriving. Gosh blame it!

Friday, September 1, 1939*†

I have been reading about the [World War I] dead and am thinking how awful it must be for a mother—or a father—to know their grown son dead. After bearing and bringing through childhood to the prime of his life a son—to find that all this is futile, that all this is ended—all vain. That he died before he began to be himself. To lose a child must be in a deep sense far worse than to lose a husband. It must make one lose the sense of continuity. A husband dead means that you are, in a way, dead—but to lose a child means you lose immortality—that you shall not go on.

Monday, September 11, 1939

I think children are our only real immortality. In them, some part of us has continuity. Shakespeare in one of his sonnets implies this. I remember when I wished to die a virgin; perhaps that would have assured me of complete mortality. That was only a little more than a year ago. Perhaps a year. Before I took Bi Sci, Mr. Mayfield said, I remember, that only the cells with [certain] chromosomes are even potentially immortal. Though I believe in a physical immortality—if it is only the conservation of matter. Perhaps the spirit hovers over the matter it inhabited. Or is broken up and distributed and never wholly reassembled identically again? Who knows? *Qui sabit*. [One thousand] years is a short time. Give Cicero a chance.

---

*The entries from August 5, 1939, through December 6, 1940, are from Joan's creative writing journal. The diary volume between those dates is missing.

†Ironically, Joan wrote this entry before she knew World War II had begun on this day.

Sunday, September 17, 1939
Immortality

How we cling at immortality! A strange sort of immortality—not so much afraid of losing our own identity as of being forgotten. How we fear to pass through the world and not leave a trace! I remember once I wanted to plant a peach tree, that it might live and bloom when I was dead. Something I should leave behind me, to live when I am gone. Funny, but the continuance of my "Aunt Polly" column in the paper—the school paper—fills me with the same sort of feeling. At first I was angry that someone should take my place, but now I see that I am not important—and that its continuance is important to me. That people may read it one day and say, "I wonder who the first Aunt Polly was." "She was." See, a piece of immortality—trite though it may seem. A peach tree—living after one. That is why people are always leaving their names everywhere. Spelled onto old school desks, carved into trees—everywhere we put it—on walls of houses where we dwelt—that posterity may look and see and know we passed. We are afraid of being lost, of being forgotten, of not leaving a trace. . . .

And yet if all man and his works were fled from the Earth, what difference on this orb would show to the observer on Mars? The polar caps would shrink and reappear and over all would roll the tides. We have traces only for ourselves. Some future though may see and half-remember . . . that we passed.

Friday, November 3, 1939

It was the day after we repealed the arms embargo. I had gone to the Blackstone library to exchange a few books. With the *Wild Swans at Coole** in my hand I walked up to the great globe that stands in the window. Ferns stood about on the floor in great pots. I turned the globe to Europe and noted that the ocean was grey-green, not blue as in the newer terrispheres. Europe fell crosswise under my fingers and, tip-toeing, I traced the worldly boundaries. I could see France and Germany on either side of the line and realized that my finger was placed on the tingling western front. That was the border when Caesar wrote his *Commentaries.* My eyes went upward and I saw in black letters—"Prussia"—this must be an old globe, I thought. Then I saw "Austro-Hungarian Monarchy." There is a name I have not seen upon a map before. I was born after the redivision of 1921. The borders of old Prussia look much like the borders of Greater Germany today. I see the Danube and—remember we have just been studying the barbarian invasions—I see "German East Africa."

They are beginning to turn out the lights in the library. Reflected in the window, I could see the interior of the room. The great globe, the tall ferns, the man reading, the shelves of books, myself on tiptoe. A sort of realization of changelessness pierces me. I am magnetized by the globe, I cannot draw my hand from the Danube. I seem to see a million people standing on the shining terrisphere, shouting to me that nothing changes. All the people who ever lived are telling me. Black specks on the globe.

---

*By William Butler Yeats.

We have just repealed the arms embargo. Of course we have—nothing ever changes. I draw my hand from the globe and it turns slowly. I watch it in the window.

I check my books and walk out between the pillars. The light from the street lamp slants through them. In the windless air, I can feel the stagnation of eternity. I can hear my footsteps beneath me and see the dry red leaves on the ground. A dog barks as I turn in at my door.

December 1939

d never get there. Tuesday Be
Wednesday, Purr, Thursday
Dixa Jobbe. I swore no one
was to stop me today. First
Gloria came along + we both
must act love thing. Poor
Gloria. But she departed
at over there without her +
just as I was slipping int
Phy Sci I heard her lit
voice "Joan". But I was late
and dragged her back with
me ... and her friend to
some girl who had a couch
seat already. Then Bill
in and sat down next
me. Steven on was very
today — Funny and goof
he poured carbon diox
(you couldn't see it) into
a paper bag + it went
It was spooky. Other e
with gasses too. (He's so
clad. Yesterday he le
Bunsen Burner co

1940

 ## Age 17

"London is Troy tonight. . . . Berlin is Troy too."

Spring 1940

*"Pity for the World"**

Prologue: Childhood

Part I: Girlhood

Part II: Premonition of war

Part III: War

Epilogue: After war

Disillusion . . .

Editor's note—The haze of a dream is over the tapestry of my life . . .

Remembered Illusion

---

*This outline appears to be for a poem or a play, but the work itself was not found.

Tuesday, August 6, 1940

I've been remembering how last year before war came there still was the half-hope that war would not come. And now all the brave words are rotten and we know we were fools to believe them and I know the words are rotten and illusions that lie.

Thursday, October 10, 1940*

To Those of My Time

You, you of my generation, you will understand what it is like. The old folks may nod and go on as they will and the younger folks—well, God knows what there is for them! But as for ourselves, we are a race apart. I mean all of us—born into this time in any country—young men in Germany and girls there too, youth in England—in China—in Scandinavia—France—all

---

*Joan wrote this entry after a month of the blitz in London and other parts of England.

over the world. You are my people—women, brothers of my time, and I love you. Born at the end of one disastrous war and bred between two wars with always the foreknowledge of this war that is come upon us as we reach adulthood. Yes, we are a race apart. Something quite different. I do not think we would any of us for all our talking fit into another time—another century, even another decade.

From our first years on, we have faced peculiar situations, and they have formed our characters within us. Those first years—most of us were born after the First World War—they were the years when our grownups had found that illusions were a lie and that revenge was the only answer to offense. That was with nations—but with people it was something newer. They all had the awful feeling of being "timed"—that they must hurry and gobble life or it would leave them. There were scandals and divorces and flat-chested women and bobbed hair. A lot of tinkling songs and a lot of money and hurry, hurry all over the world. That was the world we were born into, my friends. Children were not in place there and though most of us were loved, we were, most of us, lucky not to be abortions. Through our infancy and childhood—those first years, there was a breathless prosperity—a speed of living.

Most of us can remember running out on back porches to see an airplane going by. Most of us can remember like a story book, not so much the event as people talking about it, when Lindy flew the Atlantic. The first home radios and the first in-door beds—those were part of our childhood. City apartments and refrigerators and janitors sprinkling the lawns on summer evenings. Roller skates and tricycles and funny papers. Sure, we all remember them.

Then 1929—I guess we all remember the Depression, that's not hard. Just as we were passing out of childhood—into girlhood—boyhood—came the crash—and a lot of people committed suicide and a lot more moved into furnished rooms the way we did. I guess there was nothing unusual in that, was there? 1929, 1930, 1931, 1932. We were getting used to buying second day bread and skimmed milk by then, weren't we? Once the older part of the city was just as interesting as the newer to the kids on scooters and roller skates. I think it was sort of good for us all we got poor right then. We might have grown up thinking the whole world was made up of buildings on a quiet street with refrigeration and steam heat. I guess a lot more than my family warmed their water on a coal stove and bathed in a great iron pan.

And then, as childhood definitely ended and the youth years came on, we began to climb slowly, didn't we? On through high school and the delightful first years of that, economic conditions were steadily getting better—weren't they? I guess a whole lot of you bought your own clothes by working Saturdays besides me. I guess we were all healthier then, too. We didn't have that robust health they had in 1890 and I guess a lot more than I have something in their lungs that has to be X-rayed and checked on. I guess more than a few of us had the coughs and still have them after those lean years.

But we had a kind of brittle strength they didn't have before. A kind of body made of muscle and bone and not much else. Strong in a fragile way almost and enduring more than the weightier people of days past. We could survive on little food because we had lived that way. Oh yes—our teeth were good and our hair was soft and shining and we had good skin and lean bodies and that restless strength, but, through the faces of most of us, you could see the skull, the death that is in man, showing through. Our bones were all perilously near the surface. But we were pretty good-looking, weren't we?

Oh you, my generation!—we were a lovely lot! Sharp minds—arguing all the time and brittle bodies and even more brittle laughter—and all the time knowing that we were growing up to die. Because we weren't fooled, you know. All through those bright-colored years of adolescence we knew we were growing up to disaster. For at least four years—well, three, before it happened, we knew it was coming. Some sort of inner sense of war lay upon us. We were pretty brave—we joked about it the way we joked about love and about the polio epidemic when we were all scared to death of it. I remember getting up early one bright cold morning to hear the coronation of King George. I guess a lot of you did that too. As I remember that was May 12, 1937. We were in our early teens then. I guess that was about the time Mussolini took Ethiopia and most of us renewed our acquaintance with that faery-tale capital Addis Ababa. Still sounds like the Arabian nights, doesn't it?

The year past and they found that stuff in my lungs and maybe in some of yours too. But we joked about Arizona and read *The Magic Mountain** and worked on the school paper. We had got acclimated to the world by that time. It began to be a pretty swell place. None of us wanted to go back and live over the past years and we weren't in any hurry to get to the future.

But it was rushing on anyhow. We ignored it for a while and, I guess, for a while in those days while we were climbing out of the Depression and getting comfortable we thought we had captured the peace of prewar days. Some sort of dreamy

---

*A 1924 novel by the German writer Thomas Mann, about a sanatorium in the Swiss Alps for tubercular patients. Arizona, known for its dry climate, also attracted tubercular patients.

sunlight hit us for a while. Maybe it's true what they say about sunspots causing this war and all. Anyhow they were nice sunspots we had that year—and the next too.

I can remember walking to school in the fall of 1938. The leaves were crisp and swirled in the wind as they fell. The strong September sunlight made pretty patterns on the sidewalk. It was fun just to walk along thus—book under one arm, kicking the leaves—glad the past was over and in no hurry to get to the future. I guess in those days we were almost a real generation. I guess we almost captured an eternal feeling then—a feeling that we *belonged*—that we weren't the mistake of 1920—an overlooked abortion. Life was pretty good in the present then. Christmas and the soft powdery snow falling and melting as it fell. New Year's 1939 . . . we had the feeling of captured mortality then. We knew it wouldn't last, but we were buying into it while we could, the way those disillusioned people in the [19]10's clung to life.

I remember the summer of 1939 quite clearly. After all, it was not so long ago, was it? I was away then, working at a children's camp in Michigan, and the world had achieved standstill. It was a beautiful summer, the corn grew tall and the purple silk fluttered in the breeze as you passed the cornfields. Tall sweet stacks of hay lay in every farmyard and the crisp apples and soft-haired peaches were large and ripe. The night before the war broke out, I walked one of the farm girls home and came back [on] the road alone. There was a full yellow moon—harvest moon I guess—and the fields shimmered and danced in its light. Great leaf-shadows lay on the ground and I walked slowly as if caught by magic. The spell of the end of summer—the Dipper poured mystery into the shadowy sky. We didn't know that night that death was being written across another sky. Death, giant death for everyone.

But when, next morning, we found out, somehow we weren't surprised. Somehow it had come. The future had suddenly arrived and became the present. We went home the next day—I guess a lot of you were getting back to the city over that Labor Day weekend. Home to a war.

My mother and I went to New York then for a few days and I remember sitting awake at night in the coach. The red furnaces of Pittsburgh flashed by and someone got on the train with a red headline "France Declares War." Two fellows sitting near me began to talk. "We'll be over there in a year or two." One year's gone now. They were part of you—of me—of my generation. All of you are part of me—and I am part of you. These years we have lived through are part of us too—they have formed themselves indelibly into our separate characters. We must be thankful—for they have made us individual—a generation apart. We were on the idle hill of summer as it says in the poem* and we heard the call. Soon, no doubt, we shall answer. Without illusion, without pride or hope of glory, we shall probably answer. Let us pray to the God that we do not believe in, that at least, if we are devoid of other things, we may also be devoid of hate—for if we who have grown up so peculiarly can hate, there is no hope for the brighter world. Even we in our disillusion tell the younger children tales and beliefs we do not have.

I think the next generation will be sentimental, perhaps even chivalrous. It will not be so bad if they are. It is we who are apart. I wonder if we should have any children. Perhaps it is our younger brothers and sisters who must carry on the world. Perhaps it is we who shall destroy the old world—so that they shall have fresh beginnings for the bright world we

*Part XXXV from *A Shropshire Lad* by A. E. Housman.

do not believe in—but tell them to. It would not be good for us to carry on as we are. We are not fit.

Now it is 1940. The long awaited and prophesied death year. It is almost over. It is midnight in the autumn of 1940 as I write. The poplar leaves crunch under the foot when one walks and the chilly winds are here already. Far away a street car grinds and a child cries. London is being bombed. [Nineteen forty] is almost over. Perhaps the call shall not be issued to us—perhaps there shall be no great disaster for the strange generation in America—perhaps 1940 shall sound off an uncalling bugle and our generation in America shall grow old—have babies and rear them and live in the suburbs and die of heart failure and cancer.

But I do not think so—

Of course, none of this is true—every generation thinks itself peculiar and at the peak of the world—the last of one time—or the beginning of the next. Only because this is *my* generation do I write this about us. . . .

Bye—

Keep a tongue in your cheek.

Friday, December 6, 1940

Went to the TB place this afternoon. Dr. Freilich came out and waved at me and asked heartily how school was—I had a colored doctor this time though, as he had to go. Saw my X-rays—they looked O.K. to me, but the report said striations and something suspicious in the right apex—whatever that may be. He had me breathe and I wheezed away. Didn't tell him about my cough. It makes it too important. I gained ¼ pound—104½ now. He said, "You're getting stouter."

In the X-ray I saw something that looked like my heart—I thought, "God!" It must be made of stone to show up in my

X-ray! But then I looked closer and realized it was my locket hanging by a tiny chain over my shadowy flesh. The doctor and I both laughed, but I was struck by it. The delicate bones encased in the film of flesh—so transient—and the tiny metal chain and heart were the only real thing. I thought of those skeletons of stone-age men you see in the museum as they were found—with their jewelry still on them. And I saw I was only a skeleton in jewelry—only the jewelry of metal will outlast the jewelry of red and white. Oh heart! Oh life! Oh world so soon to pass! I want to die young (though I think if I were assured of that, I would be afraid of nothing). Well, one's life is still one's own—to take. . . . The doctor told me to eat a lot and come back in a month.

I was thinking about Larry* and me on the streetcar today. Somehow in denying outwardly we had met before that Thursday, we admitted each other, we admitted that moment to a greater importance than it had before—than it should have had. We were so superbly modern—but for a moment when our jaws fell and our eyes burned into each other, we were superbly elemental.

Again we showed civilization our good breeding—the modern world in us that Saturday night when he came and sat by me. He had been drinking (well, at least he wasn't drunk that night with me) and his eyes were bloodshot slightly and there was a cigaret in my hand—the black sleek dress on me—the modern fluffy bangs . . . our constrained jesting way. We were both trying to throw off a puzzling sloth. Somehow in denying each other, we admitted each other. Oh world—Oh delightful! amazing! constraining! yet still exciting modern

---

*Larry Johns appears on a list of boyfriends Joan created in 1943.

world! It's nice to give your age as 17—somehow it immediately forgives you many things.

P.S. I was moaning to Betty about how they all go off their nuts when they meet me—Dik* certainly departed from the normal—he got mad and I thought suddenly, "The world's too big to pass for a dream"—anyhow, he parted from the normal—he's never returned to that sweet abnormal (for him) state again—and Larry, well, he certainly acted strange on the roof. I wouldn't call that kiss—that conversation—conventional. They all go off their little beams. Betty thinks it's better that way. She wishes they did that for her. But I don't know. She says I'm the type they like to cuddle. God, I'm the intellectual type—as you undoubtedly know. Anyhow, that's what I'd say. Well, I don't know whether it's better or not they go nuts when they meet me—but at least it makes life interesting.

Me with my gamine face [and] irregular bangs . . .

Saturday, December 7, 1940

Hello, darling—well, here I am, back from the barn dance. It was in a barn full of horses and smelt and we stole ham and ate it as is—naked† in the car—no bread or anything. Marshall and Betty sat in front with Frank, the driver (poor boy), and Bob and I and Bert (who just came from France this fall—he saw the fall of Paris—I asked him if it was exciting and he said, "No, Paris was declared an open city") sat in the back and sang symphony music and camp songs.

---

*Dik Edwards also appears on her boyfriend list.
†The ham was naked; the people were not.

Tuesday, December 10, 1940

Norm said he always felt gloomy and I said I did sometimes too, but, when I looked in the mirror when I felt my worst, I always laughed 'cause I knew it couldn't be *that* bad.

Oh god! Am I the *cuddly* type? As Betty declares? She's been out with Norm and it didn't happen. . . . You know, it's sort of gloomy when you think of it—the way they all say, "Well, we're going to war next year anyhow so let's have a little fun now."

Oh, world, Good Night!

Wednesday, December 11, 1940

Hello dear—well, well—I never felt so peacefully, passionately finished with anything. Dik Edwards. A nauseating dope. He and Betty and Ginny and Norm were playing bridge together in the C-Shop* when I came in this afternoon. I sat there and knitted and after a while Norm said, "Oh, do you two know each other?"

And Dik said, "No."

And Norm looked at me and I shook my head no.

And he introduced "Dik Edwards, Joan Wehlen," and Dik softly smiled as though remembrance was recurring to him and said, "I'm glad to meet you, Joan."

And I only nodded. It was as though we had never met before—the first time I had seen him. After all, we never would have met if it had not been for a mere slip of mine in being half an hour late one night—meeting him this way in the C-Shop, I would not have thought of him twice.

---

*Coffee Shop, on the University of Chicago campus.

All, all definitely over . . . not even resentment—just dullness. I never thought I could say his name so passively, "Dik Edwards"—to think the chink of falling icicles and the click of my high heels used to say "Dik, Dik" to me.

[Written between Wednesday, December 11, and Friday, December 13, 1940]

Went to German Christmas party last night—Santa Claus, a pretty tree, marzipan that I like, etc. Betty came too. They sang German Christmas carols, "O Tannenbaum." We joked about it sounding like a Bund* meeting and Betty wanted to get up and shout, "We're all Americans!" But we mustn't even pretend to have that kind of patriotism. God, keep us wise and cool.

Then they sang—a male quartet—old songs in the faintly meaningful language (I can understand about one quarter) . . . and I leaned back dreamily. I like to hear their strong male voices—deep and proud—singing the good songs. Schubert—"Silent Night" . . . the tree brings out the Nordic, the Scandinavian, in me and I think of my ancestors. Betty whispers, "What an ugly language it is!" The world's spinning outside, the moon is gleaming on the white snow. In here we are separate . . . warm—out of the world. Someone opens a window and a chilly blast sweeps in.

Herr Jolles sees me and nods, smiling. He makes an announcement and it is only afterwards I learn he has said the punch is spilled. My German is none too good. But the almond paste cookies are. I eat a great many. Betty says, "Let's go"—we go—just as Santa Claus returns . . . with

---

*An American Nazi organization.

bells. Someone stops me at the door and says, "Are you a high school girl?"

I say with dignity, "A University woman."

Herr Jolles looks up laughing and recognizes me, "Oh, yes, indeed she is," he corroborates. "But aren't you going to stay? No? Then *Gute Nacht*."

Young men like him . . . they are all killing . . . lots of them, all over . . .

Betty and I race over the cold, gleaming Midway. Our breath curls in the air. The white clouds, like curly feathers, seem to be behind the moon. Orion is a fantastic diamond necklace in the sky. We dance in the dark at her house: the Conga. Do our Sociology: Hobbes, Locke.* God, this is 1940 AD. Good Night, World!

Monday, December 16, 1940

Oh, this is delightful—my quarterlies,† I'm sure I've flunked. Made sandwiches at YWCA. Betty and I can't understand how our appetites have gone down. We only ate two sandwiches and spoonfuls of tuna fish and milk each. We can't understand it.

Then to *Maroon* meeting.‡ I wore my overalls and plaid flannel shirt. Everybody socked their heads when they saw me. Chet said, "Do you think you're still in Michigan?" and Charles Darrough (he's growing a beard again) said I'm not the outdoor type. Dan Megley said the *Maroon* sure will be

---

*Thomas Hobbes, the English philosopher, wrote *The Leviathan*; John Locke was a philospher, political theorist, and physician.
†Her exams.
‡The student newspaper of the University of Chicago.

a good paper now. Everybody cheery. Then studies. In Sosh*
Commons room took off our shoes and tapped walls for secret
panels like little monkeys and then recited Napoleon's exploits
and sprawled like alligators.

Tonight I suddenly realized Larry and I were over . . . had
been over in my mind for sometime. There were no unfin-
ished ends left for us. No idea of meeting again. It's O.K. I
was just surprised I realized it—

Tuesday, December 17, 1940

Well, I won't be 17 much longer—three more days—then
adulthood. After all, 18, in the sight of the state I am grown,
self-responsible. The Kappes called up tonight—en masse—
to make sure I was coming Friday night. They must be having a surprise for my birthday. Paul† spoke. Gee, I remember
when the sight of him would set me atingling—the Greek
God. Well, time passes—that's sure all over. These things
that have happened to me this quarter will be over like that
too. After all—it's only a quarter of a school semester. Not
quite three months—

> Time like an ever-deepening stream
> Bears all his sons away
> They fly forgotten as a dream
> Flies at the break of day.‡

So has flown my past—all our pasts—I was thinking:
1940 is almost over . . . the magic year—the death year. Our

---

*Sociology.
†Paul Kappe's nickname was the Greek God. His brother, Eddie,
appears on the boyfriend list.
‡Here Joan paraphrased the hymn "Our God, Our Help in Ages Past."

youth-year. We'll look back and say, "Life was exciting when we were young." It was. The magic years, though, are always magic. I'm glad I was young in 1940. Soon Larry, Dik will be "last year" . . . part of the past of the sister-years.

Norm Foster called up tonight to take me to the Kappa Sig Christmas party—tomorrow night. God, I never thought he'd ask me out again after the way I treated him! The knitting needles! . . . Well, anyhow, he did.

Douglas can't understand why I'm so sweet. . . . I can't either. I positively drip with sugar when I'm around him.

P.S. FDR wants us to rent our arms to the British. Our arms! Pretty soon we'll be renting our boys—but we'll never get *them* back.

Wednesday, December 18, 1940

Oh, world—the years so quickly gone—all the nice boys with the nice shadows in their faces . . . the war could kill them all—

Friday, December 20, 1940

Well, life, dear life, is always interesting and full of hectic surprises! Which is not original but just the same true. Anyhow—guess who's 18 today—what young lady has just come of age? Me, "Miss Joan Wehlen—18." There is only one thing: you can be forgiven things at 17 you can't be forgiven at 18. Larry mustn't happen again.

Anyhow—oh, after seven years—since I was in grammar school—the old "Greek God" of my prehistoric era, he has finally discovered me. When that is gone forever from me. Said he leaning across the table to me: "You know, I've been an awful fool . . . not to have paid more attention to you. I never noticed you were so beautiful—such pretty eyes. . . ." It was like words out of a past that had no meaning any longer. I said, "I suppose you know you've broken my heart."

You see after my class today, I went up to St. Peter's for the Xmas party. Got there early and made up—mascara and all—listened to choir and radio in Henry's room. He was quite hospitable. Then upstairs . . . Eddie came in with my birthday present. "Wifey," he said, "here." He still has that strange physical attraction for me. Remember my last birthday. . . . I had resolved yesterday morning to let him kiss me if I had the chance, but after what happened last night I didn't take the chance. I enjoyed getting it though. Wait, later I'll tell you about last night—Oh!

Anyhow, Eddie came over to the stairs where I was sitting and said he wanted a Christmas present too and we were all joking and then suddenly he said softly, "Joan," and I thought, How cute, and lifted my eyes and face with that all come on, soft-lipped look, and he staggered across the room. It was fun. Everybody put their arms around me and I was waltzing around starved to death.

Then Eddie and I went upstairs to fix hot chocolate. I began to eat a donut—I hadn't had any supper. The powdered sugar settled on the floor in a cloud. Eddie came over to where I was standing and put his arms around me. I can't help it— the touch of him still attracts me—even if I were repelled in every other way. He put one hand low on my waist and the other close on my shoulders and drew me to him. It's only the touch that draws me—nothing else—but it sure draws me.

But not hard enough. I wiggled and took a huge bite of donut just before he could kiss me. "I'm starved," I said cheerily and walked away. The powdered sugar swirled all over. I went downstairs. Murmured, "I'm starved," several times in a winsome voice and Bob Barnes was going to take me out to get something to eat. We went up to get my coat and found Eddie who had opened the door and reproached me for my unfaithfulness.

Then home about 2:10 or so. Dale and I this time in the back and he put his arm around me, held my hand and we talked. You know, Betty thinks it's some yielding way of mine that lures them on. For they all come on. Dale was no exception. But it wasn't my fault. We were sitting in the back . . . he let his arm hold my shoulder and pressed my hand. We talked. He was born in France. All the sudden I looked up and his face was looming before me slightly bent as they do so as not to kiss head on. I ducked and did hair-in-the-face. And looked at the lake feeling suddenly sad. Talked on as if nothing had happened. Again. This time he tilted my face up by the chin and said, "Why do you turn away when I want to kiss you?" And I said simply, "To stop you." And he tried again and kissed the silky hair over my ear.

Just as we got to my house, he laid his hand on my cheek and turned my face to his and said, "I'm not [going] to force you—just leave my hand there." He laid it on my smooth, cool cheek.

And I said, "I know you're not," and left it.

Also left the car then. Betty stayed overnight with me and we discussed men and held a postmortem.

Woke up this morning thinking of his hand on my cheek. Norm called to take me out tonight. I said I had another engagement already. Riding on the streetcar, [I] could think of nothing but my sins which had brought on my fate—but exciting—that yielding, soft-lip look—Betty wishes they'd tried it on her.

Wednesday, December 25—Christmas Day 1940

Hello—isn't that a lovely, peculiar, definitely one-of-a-kind dateline. It's afternoon now, about four o'clock. Mom and Dad have gone to the races and I'm waiting for Betty to come over. A violin quartet is playing on the radio . . . "May I Never Love Again." Time is a funny mirror—it holds more things than you can see. Two people standing at different angles to the mirror see different sights—and both see the truth . . . if there is truth. It's raining outside now, a warm rain. I'm in my gold wool dress and have my hair piled high; I look quite 18. I've been coughing all afternoon. Mom got me a flannel nightie 'cause I'm always freezing and they've been calling me "Gramma" all day 'cause I don't even let them open a window anymore. I, who used to insist on two feet open in the dead of winter! They're playing "God Bless America" now.

We went to church last night. Midnight service at St. Paul's. Britain must win . . . said Mr. Belliss in substance. God Save the World. Shopping downtown yesterday—midst all the gay holly—the faery lighted castles at [Field's department store] . . . the toy windows at Mandels—all the streets lighted up and people jostling and stepping on each other's toes and saying, "Merry Christmas"—Bing Crosby singing "Adeste fideles" on *The Voice of State Street* . . . a phonograph in Woolworth's playing "Happy Birthday, Dear Jesus." Everything holiday and gay. . . .

Then on Michigan Blvd. I passed suddenly the Cunard* window. An exhibit for the BWR†—pictures of little children in Britain—homes bombed—helmets that could be knitted

---

*A British shipping company.
†British War Relief.

for the RAF—a noble purpose—but it's making war in our hearts. The little German children are bombed and hungry too. . . . And all the sudden, in an emotional intensity, I thought, "This may be the last Christmas we shall have." I should be wise and know the world will never end. . . . An unofficial truce played over Christmas in Europe today—Hitler said, "German fliers will not fly on Christmas if British fliers will not." And they did not. And so a white, bloodless Christmas there and the sky is weeping here.

In church last night, the organ was playing "Gesù bambino"* and I remembered my birthday last year—and I remembered Christmas last year. "The elusiveness, the past tense, of what has happened, the finality of each act"—and I knew that beautiful phrase of mine, for it *is* beautiful—was true. Time is a funny mirror. I regret not the past. [I] took communion. I am a hypocrite, but I am not fooling myself. They are playing, "I Dream of Jeannie with the Light Brown Hair." . . . Joan, Joan, can you be tending sheep in Domremy?† . . . The merry-go-round‡ in Benton Harbor. Funny, what strange things come back to you.

Missed the Christmas pageant at St. Peter's Sunday by oversleeping. Disappointed—I had wanted to see it from afar. I've always been in it, you know. Like life, you must be out of the pageant to see it.

---

*An Italian Christmas carol.
†From a poem by Edna St. Vincent Millay about Joan of Arc, a figure Joan long admired after first reading about her in George Bernard Shaw's play *Saint Joan*. The shared name intensified her identification with this medieval heroine.
‡Presumably at the House of David Amusement Park in Michigan, which Joan went to occasionally.

Funny, all this Christmas season, I have felt they were singing the Christmas carols to *me*—that I was Mary. When someone sang "Ave Maria," I got positively atingle. I was Mary. . . .

King George is on the radio now with his Christmas message to the British Empire. Again and again—war . . . King George asks for victory in the new year. . . .

Later Christmas Night

Well, Betty has come and gone and so has Christmas—Daddy made us both drink wine so we did and danced and lay on the sofa—the springs were terrible—Betty got caught twice!—and talked. She said if she were King George she would have broken the truce and flown right over to Germany and bombed every village and plant she could. That surprised me for she's usually pretty broad-minded. Hate has penetrated pretty far—I said I didn't agree with her but we didn't argue.

Went down to wait for Betty's mother—midnight. The man downstairs was beating his wife, or threatening to, anyhow, and the man upstairs brought a woman in with him and three drunk people came down from upstairs, and a man with a bandage on his head wandered in and out, and a woman came out on the third floor and asked us what time it was and disappeared. It was like Grand Central Station on Harper Avenue.* The man downstairs was going to throw his

---

*Sometime between September 1, 1939, and December 1940 the family moved from Cornelia Avenue on the North Side to the South Side near the University of Chicago, so that Joan wouldn't have so far to go to U-High or the University of Chicago. The exact number on Harper Avenue is not known. They later moved to 4950 South Blackstone; by 1942, they moved to 5629 South Dorchester Avenue.

wife out but stamped out himself instead, then came in the back way. Christmas night 1940—still that transitory peace flapping over Europe—the Greeks are fighting though and so are the Italians in Egypt—Aunt Sarah over tomorrow— Christmas caroling later.

Anyhow, I can hold my liquor. All except the Coke. Johnny burned me with his cigaret and then kissed it. It still hurts—

All this is tawdry but fun.

Good Night.

Friday, December 27, 1940

Hello, it's fun being alone in the house. I'm curled up on the sofa with my slender silken legs spilled beneath me. I enjoy the stage-set atmosphere of the place. The radio is pattering on and the tick-tock of the eternal clock is clicking away. It's drizzling outside—about 8:30, I should say. Mom and Dad have gone out. I wish somebody would call, I want to go out New Year's Eve. Life is so placid tonight. Tick-tock, says the clock cheerily. Stopped in at International House [this] after-noon. Everybody knitting for BWR. Anne's knitted three sweaters. God Save the World. It's a war play on now . . . a German and an Englishman are talking to each other on Christmas Eve—about to die. God, God save the world.

And now good-bye—

Saturday, December 28, 1940

I was reading my new book of poems tonight . . . "Ye Mari-ners of England" and Goldsmith's "The Deserted Village"— Byron's "There was a sound of revelry by night" and all the poems we are used to and suddenly I realized: the world's not going to come back the way it was. . . . Oh yes, the world is changing . . . sleep, children, sleep . . . the world's changing.

Troy—who thinks of Troy now. London is Troy tonight,*
London is brave somehow—burning and huddled in shelters, yet walking also in the unlighted streets. . . . London is
Troy. Everyone is wrong, nobody is right: Berlin is Troy too
. . . Paris is fallen. Where is Helen? There is no Helen, only
democracy is our maid . . . democracy. The maiden some
went to rescue, but to avoid being hampered by her in the
ensuing fight, split her breast with a sword. Democracy, the
maid, is lying dead somewhere on the battlefield. Oh, world!

We were sitting in the living room tonight, Mom and I,
she sewing and I knitting, listening to a Mass of Beethoven's
and I looked up. It was perfectly still. Against the background
of the music could be heard the steady tick-tock of the clock.
The pendulum swinging gaily apparent. And I thought: no
moment comes back. This is done forever as we live. The
plain rough tweed of my skirt, the soft wool in my hands,
mother's brown hair as she sews, the square funny Victorian
rug with the printed mottos on it: "Virtue is its own reward,"
"Honesty is the best policy." Oh world, world! Every second
that the clock ticks out is gone forever in the reaches of time—
can never in any eternity be brought back. I am not sorry,
but it is so. . . . I was thinking: If I were dying, what would I
remember. . . .

The world is changing. There is a tight band around my
chest under my breasts, as though a cord were tied there. This
is physical, not psychological, and it comes oftener now. . . .
It hurts when I breathe. . . . I almost gasp as my ribs are
constricted. . . .

---

*Troy was the city besieged and then destroyed by the Greeks in the
Trojan War. Earlier, Joan describes reading *The Iliad*, Homer's epic
that describes some of the action.

It's drizzling out now. The world is changing. Henry, my old choirmaster, Thursday night, came up and put his arms around my waist, from behind me: my old choirmaster! Oh world . . .

Some thought of holding time came into my head as we sang "Auld Lang Syne" that night. I was on Johnny's lap, holding the pretty purple punch in my glass. The tree gleamed, Christmas 1940—Oh world. Johnny's arms tightened. "Hold me, but you can't hold time . . . drink the wine, once it's drunk, you drink no more." I don't mind this for myself, but it's sad to think of all the people who have lived and are dead thoroughly. . . . I like it for myself. . . .

Mom and I went downtown—shopped and saw *Love Thy Neighbor** at the Chicago. . . . Met my soul mate on the IC† on the way home. Sat in front of us. And our eyes met in the dark glass of the window. Blond, crew haircut, lean features. Once he turned around straight to look at me, as if to make sure I wasn't just a reflection. Of course, Mom chatted blithely through it all. When we got off, I looked back once after the trains started to see him inside. He was outside on the platform and grinned into my eyes. I gulped and went on listening to Mom and laughed at myself. . . .

---

*A 1940 film with Jack Benny and Fred Allen.
†IC stands for Illinois Central, the raised electric railway connecting Hyde Park, the neighborhood of the University of Chicago, with downtown Chicago.

If he start today themorrow
I know hell blow up the
building. Cant you see him
with nitro-glycerine. Oh
— dont mistake me tho — he
very brilliant.

Anyhow as we were led
"ass Bill asked me to go
and see "nature son" P-
montown next Saturday.
I blew away into the we
... And now. Often was
my own, ro day a new jar
and all. I really must
my studying.

Kenny called twinte
wanted to go out but
said I had a date
Well now,
6'night!

Sunday—December
Well baby, its come, what we
always knew would come, we
we never quite believed in.
Deathly calm about it

1941

Age 18

"Crisis with Japan, it seems."

New Year's Day 1941

Oh world, all past . . . conscription coming: we didn't believe it, did we? England standing alone. The corn silk shimmering in the breeze . . . London Bridge is falling down. . . .

This is 1941—the magic year is over. The world is going to die slowly. How quickly time passes. How slowly it drags. It passes too soon. I'm 18 now, suddenly! Christmas 1940—unofficial truce—no bombs in London or Berlin tonight. . . .

Caroling the day after Christmas. The Christmas truce is over. The pageant is over. I wasn't the Virgin this year. I shouldn't have been, it's as well. . . . Eddie. . . . The past is last year. . . . Johnny picking me up and I so light he wouldn't set me down. The wind blowing my bangs . . . Johnny kissing me under the mistletoe . . . long and hard, and yet soft. And I, surprisingly, responding.

They just had an "Aid to Britain" program on the radio. There was a New Year's truce too—Happy New Year . . .

Thursday, January 2, 1941

Well now, just think—two weeks ago today—Dale—that crazy night.* I was kissed . . . a week ago. I was kissed. That Christmas party, caroling, wine. Johnny. Well, tonight, again Thursday, I sit home. . . .

P.S. The dear children† have just come home. They're all excited and happy and had their arms full of tomato soup and steak. They won $2 on the horses. . . . Now they're in the living room buzzing about "sure systems," etc. I'm in bed with Vicks VapoRub and hot towels on my chest in a flannel nightie, trying to listen to the symphony. I feel like Gramma. They're so cute.

Sunday, January 5, 1941

Well, I've got them amused for the evening now. Excuse me, I must go in and decide a spat for them. They each accuse the other of cheating. I've just taught them bridge and now I've left them with it the way God left Adam and Eve in the garden with the apple. I feel as guilty as God about it too. But, like him, I feel that at least I've given them something to amuse themselves with. "Honeymoon Bridge" at that. First I taught Daddy and then Mom. Now they're lost. . . .

They're so cute. They bought stuff for soup and this morning I heard noises and then Mom came tramping into my room almost in tears, flourishing six beets on a stalk. "We're having an argument—I want to put beets in the soup

---

*See the entry from Friday, December 20, 1940.
†Joan's joke for referring to her parents.

and he doesn't!" she wailed. I settled it by telling her to cook the beets separately and then retreated. Life is delightful.

Tuesday, January 7, 1941

It's funny how people meet and touch and pass from each other. Like balloons, as filmy bubbles, contacting and then bouncing away . . .

P.P.S. The Italians surrendered Bardia [in Libya]—another faery-tale city—Sunday after two weeks' siege. Yesterday in his opening address to Congress, Pres. Roosevelt asked for all possible aid short of men (how?) to Britain.

Thursday, January 9, 1941

"I see London, I see France."
"I've been to London and I've seen the Queen."

And what's more, I've seen Larry! Oh! Life! Life makes you feel wretched and excited all at once. Life is fun. Life makes me sigh and I wheeze and see it's all a joke—but oh!—Larry. It was this way. Very dramatic. We're always dramatic. It was funny. Just last night I was thinking of him saying, "I'm going to teach you something," and then looking at me: "Maybe you can teach me something too." I was just thinking of that last night. . . .

Well, anyhow (that's not unusual, I still think of the dear boy now and then)—I was sitting in Harper Library where you get the books, waiting for *Madame Bovary* and listlessly looking at "*wissen, weiss, gewissen,*"* or something of the sort.

*The German principle parts for the verb "to know": *wissen* means "to know," and [*Ich*] *weiss* means "[I] know." The word *gewissen* should be the past participle *gewusst*. (German was not Joan's strongest subject, as she was first to admit!)

And an overcoat went by about 11:25. It looked a bit familiar. What was in the overcoat, I mean. I said softly, "Larry."

And he turned. "Joan."

I was sitting on the little table there and had my gold sweater on that matches my eyes. My hair was swirled up and my bangs were soft and fluffy. He came over and leaned on the table beside me. "How are you?" he asked. My heart was pounding like African tom-toms and I was sure he could hear it. It was hitting the side of my chest with tremendous force. It seemed like everyone in the room must be watching us because of our dramatic greeting. His eyes were brown today. . . . You know, after that night on the roof this was the way I imagined we'd meet some day. . . . In Harpers, suddenly, "Larry . . . Joan." Of course, since then there's been our social drama interlude and all.

Well, anyhow. You know how he is. It's not me, I'm sure, but he has a way of projecting himself into you, losing himself in you, if he's with you. Well, he did. I could feel his eyes clear through to my spinal column. We talked about Christmas, Wisconsin, my club, [how] he was going to go away for Christmas but had to work, how he was as a Freshman. He said he studied very hard then, was anti-social—the hermit soul. I said, "Well, you've changed since then, haven't you?" And he smiled into me. He lived at the Fraternity House then. I could hear my heart pounding. I was afraid Betty would come back and find us together and start scattering roses or something. Finally he had to go. He went.

I sighed deeply and watched him over my German book. He's the most elusive person. This is the first time I've seen him since the dance over a month ago. Oh—except in Harpers that night. He brought that up himself—to think he remembered. Oh! Anyhow Betty saw me peering up over my German and said, "What are you looking at" and I babbled on and she almost died. Everyone in the library must have noticed. And then he came back. Betty and I were together and he nodded and went on. Would it have been different if I were alone? Of course not. Oh, Joan. Stop being foolish. He went down the stairs with someone else and kept turning his head to look back, Betty told me, till she thought he'd fall down. I couldn't look. Then we ran into the monk's place* to watch him—running into the little one on the way. I collapsed and sighed and wheezed away. We reenacted it the way you do, you know. We really enter into things. . . .

Have just read Malthus[†]—so encouraging, you know. Well, we have birth control today. But you'd think more people would use it. Nothing can change the fact that this is lush—this is life, this is living.

Thursday, January 23, 1941
British have captured Derna.[‡] All the faery-tale cities of the world—are real . . . Derna, Tobruk. Oh world.

P.S. They reenacted the play they gave the night Lincoln was killed. I was weeping for all the people dead.

Tuesday, January 28, 1941
Hello—sold *Maroons* at the "Aid the Allies" meeting tonight. Way over a hundred—with Marshall. We had fun hawking

---

*"The monk's place" was presumably some gothic alcove in the library. Joan's German textbook contained a slip of paper on which she had written, "Betty, I'm typing in the monk's place." She must have left this message for Betty and later retrieved the paper.
[†]Thomas Robert Malthus, an English scholar of the late 18th and early 19th centuries who warned against excessive population growth.
[‡]The British actually captured Derna on January 31, 1941, but, curiously enough, Joan wrote this under January 23.

them. Sat out behind and fooled around.* I guess we were the only two people there who didn't want to "Aid the Allies"—it was horrid—all the speeches. Afterward we stood at the door as they went out. Saw Larry. I sorta started when I saw him. He was with a girl. He said, "Hello, Joan!" I said, "Oh hello, Larry," and smiled foolishly. I always act like a high-school girl expecting to be seduced when I see him. I flatter myself at that. We were discussing seduction in German today and I've been reading *Ulysses*—maybe that's why. Marshall was quite nice.

Saturday, February 1, 1941

Tonight went out with Neil. Went to dance at the Y—to see *Kitty Foyle* downtown—ate dinner at 2 AM. Went to Cocktail Lounge. I wasn't having a very good time. I usually do, you know. In the darkness of the cocktail lounge, I smoked a cigaret in silence, sipped red wine, and thought to myself: "I'm not having a good time, why not let him kiss me and give him a good time at least." It was cold-blooded kindness: I wanted him to have a good time.

Sunday Morning, February 2, 1941

Hello. Have just finished [*An*] *Enemy of the People*.† Fell asleep reading it last night. The figure of Dr. Stockmann for a time seemed unbelievable to me. Unbelievable because I could not think there were men that brave. And then I thought of Lindbergh. . . .

---

*"Fooling around" had a nonsexual connotation at this time.
†A play by Henrik Ibsen; Dr. Stockmann risks ostracization by speaking the truth.

Lindbergh,* our beloved Lindy of days now gone. I remember standing on the back porch as a little girl to see his plane go by . . . 1927. Then, those dreadful days of the kidnapping . . . Lindy, our hero. The pictures in the paper of the blonde, curly-headed little Lindy that was to be the future, that was to carry on the Lindberghs: blowing out the candles on his first birthday cake. And later the crumpled decayed remains of him, with the tangled yellow hair still shining. The electrocuted Hauptmann—with a little boy looking like the little Lindbergh. All that sorrow. I suppose in the old days, so many children died that one's death was not noted—but now. Oh yes, though, think of little Astyanax† thrown from the wall at Troy.

We have our epic too—this, the Epic of Lindbergh. And now after all these years, he speaks the truth—the truth to us. And we call our beloved Lindy "an enemy of the people." Only two weeks ago he spoke to the House on the war. He thinks

---

*Charles Lindbergh, the first man to fly solo across the Atlantic, represented the energy of the Roaring '20s as a heroic aviator. Several years after he married Anne Morrow, their one-year-old son was kidnapped and killed. Much controversy still swirls around the trial of the child's murderer. After his famous feat and tragic personal life, Lindbergh made news in the late 1930s and early 1940s by adhering to the principles of the America First Committee's isolationist policies. His actions came to be seen as unpatriotic and apologetic to Hilter and fascism. Joan was against joining the war on different principles. She agreed with the tenets of pacifism as espoused by the president of the University of Chicago, Robert Maynard Hutchins, who had a vexed relationship with the America First Committee (though Hutchins never joined the America First Committee and denied being isolationist).

†The son of the dead Trojan hero, Hector, is killed by the Greeks.

it's better if no one wins the war—if it is stopped immediately. Oh truth. And we revile him and call him "Fifth Columnist,"* etc. Well, in the long run, our blonde-headed Siegfried hero Lindbergh will *be* the Legend. We shall remember him. Or others shall. . . .

And was remembering last Tuesday, when Dale and I were selling papers at the "Aid the Allies" meeting, he laid his head in my lap and said, "Joan, you're so sweet"—and I was suddenly struck by revulsion. He was getting people to sign an "Aid the Allies" petition.

Sunday Evening, February 2, 1941, 11:00

Yesterday went to *Maroon* dinner—heard Hutchins.† He looked as if he was in pain, but he was rather witty. Said the chances were 10 to 1 for us getting in war. Quite jolly. [Found my book on Virgil and thought about] what passed between Dido and Aeneas in the underworld. A piece of paper slipped out—the French army marching through blooming orchards last spring in Flanders. Here and there with my assignments were notes: "Germans in France" . . . "Calais has fallen" . . . "Belgium surrendered." It was moving rather fast last spring. The world against the world that was . . . new patterns. Another picture slipped out . . . a German soldier and a girl in a Berlin night-club. I guess life always goes on . . . even in Troy.

---

*A Fifth Columnist is someone suspected of being a traitor.
†Robert Maynard Hutchins, president of the University of Chicago.

Sunday, February 9, 1941

Dennis can't go on with his flying now 'cause he's not a citizen. Dennis, a foreigner. Dennis, English. Winston Churchill spoke over the radio today.* I heard him. Pigface.

Wednesday, February 12, 1941

Hello! Well, [it's] Lincoln's birthday. Stayed home alone and read *Das Abenteuer der Neujahrsnacht*† for German. Heard Willkie‡ on radio tonight. Wants lots of aid to Britain . . . Gabriel Heatter.§ He always has that way of making you think "Tonight's the night—these are the days." Anyhow, Franco has just met Mussolini [and] is to meet Marshal Petain tomorrow. Rumors of peace between Italy and Britain. Italy badly needs it—or so we're told. 'Nuff of Europe.

Flunked my German test—F. That's bad, you know. Hitler would be disappointed. He'd better put off the invasion for a while.

P.S. Jim Burns had a breakdown, Dik told us, and is in Florida recuperating. I wonder if it's his ulcers. You know he's going to die. The poor boy—and we were so impatient with him for not enjoying life.

Well, I still do.

---

*He gave one of his most famous speeches, in which he said, "Give us the tools, and we will finish the job." Read the transcription of the speech at http://www.ibiblio.org/pha/policy/1941/1941-02-09a.html.
†By Heinrich Zschokke.
‡Wendell Willkie was the Republican nominee for president in 1940, running against the incumbent Franklin Delano Roosevelt. He lost to Roosevelt, but he later became his representative. He traveled around the world on behalf of the United States.
§A radio commentator and announcer.

Sunday, February 16, 1941

Went to movie with Betty [for] free. Saw *Arise, My Love**— about the recent events—Warsaw burning—Paris fallen— peace in Compiègne . . . sad—comedy . . .

Wednesday, February 19, 1941

Hullo!—saw Cricket again today. Was coming out of C-Shop with Dougie and Betty. Had been practicing my new personality on him. It consists of looking superior and uttering "huh" at intervals instead of giggling youthfully. The only trouble is that when I hear myself grunting like an Indian I have to giggle helplessly so the prime purpose is destroyed. I also have my bangs up now and look quite superior with my high forehead. Anyhow, I was coming out of the C-Shop with my coat over my shoulders when someone grabbed the arm of it and almost dragged it off.

P.S. My reformation began yesterday. Study instead of C-Shop in afternoon. I'm trying to make it gradual though. Had medical at Billings [Hospital] today—102 lbs—disgustingly healthy.

Thursday, February 20, 1941

Cartoon in paper of 1919—Lloyd George and company leaving Versailles—a baby labeled class of 1940 is crying in a dark corner. Asks L. George, "What's that crying?" How prophetic—that's me—the class of '40.

---

*This 1940 film starred Claudette Colbert and Ray Milland; Billy Wilder was among the film's screenwriters.

Saturday, February 22, 1941

And now—the world:

Japan—US crisis—mebbe war, they say.
King Alfonso reported dead.[*]
Air battle over English Channel.
And now—from me—G'night!

Saturday, March 1, 1941

Hullo. Forgot to tell you that when I walked to the streetcar yesterday afternoon after leaving Hugh, I saw the big black headlines: "Nazis in Rumania." This morning they said "Bulgaria Signs Axis Treaty" and this afternoon "German Forces in Bulgaria." Planes droning over Sofia[†] now. British are expected to break relations with Bulgaria tomorrow. It's dawn in Europe now, a grey sun rising over grey-red lands, tinting the mountain peaks rosy, but leaving the valleys still in shadow. Dawn in Europe.

Hugh, shall I describe Hugh to you in an unpleasant sense—to relieve my soul and the way I will forget to look at him, that is nonetheless true. He carries his glasses instead of wearing them and is forever squinting near-sightedly up at things and people. He has a funny way of walking and his toes turn out, but we dance delightfully together. He's stoop-shouldered and he doesn't look at you when he's talking and he has rather hollow cheeks. His hair is non-descript and his eyes are light. He is almost pale. He has a full lower lip to redeem his face from cold intellectuality and almost

---

[*]The Spanish king was in exile and actually did not die until a week later.
[†]The capital of Bulgaria.

make it sensuous. I would imagine he'd look bad in a bathing suit. . . .

When he talks he reminds me greatly of the Fog* which should make me greatly ware but rather illogically increases my tenderness. For a month after I met him I thought not of him—so this gets something off my mind—but I still think I would like him a lot. I hope I don't.

P.S. Blackouts in Bulgaria tonight and British Chutists landing in Italy.

Monday, March 3, 1941

Dear, cancel everything from last night. I'm happy again with my true love. He has just walked me home through freezing blasts and I feel like Buck in *The Call of the Wild*†—ready to die for a good master—also I'm wheezing so I probably will. Also freezing. Then to Hanley's. Sat on leather set and drank red wine and (I had had no supper again) Hugh and I shared [a] huge hot dog. They were playing "The Last Time I Saw Paris"—oh! Hugh started murmuring about if he could get a car but it got no further. I fear it won't either. Then home freezing. Fun. Sang "La Marseillaise" on the empty icy street of Blackstone. Russia has just entered Bulgaria. Hugh will be dead in 40 years.

Tuesday, March 4, 1941

Woof, woof, here's your little Russian wolfhound again—or was it an Eskimo dog last time? Anyhow, here I am, happy and, strange to say, not feeling very healthy. You don't suppose I have pleurisy? Everything through my ribs from my

---

*Joan's nickname for another boy.
†A novel by Jack London.

waist to my trachea feels as if it's tied in knots. I've been gasping away on my back for an hour. Otherwise, though, darling, I feel fine, in spite of German test and all.

Do you suppose life, after all, was merely a mistake, a sport, that appeared in a universe destined to be non-organic—and that it will play itself out in a while. And things will go on again . . . inorganic? It's an idea—hadn't occurred to me before. I was reading the words in Cobb Hall and I looked up and around, trying to visualize the world. The blue light fell from the white-flecked sky on the stone building. A faint lazy snow was falling. The heads of the boys and girls around me, bent in study. We seemed so immensely present—so full of our lives. The shock of the new idea was strong yet. "Of course," I thought, looking around, "Of course the universe was meant for bugs like us!" But the idea that it might not be had offered itself. *Was* the universe made for us, made for life, or are we only here, by freak's grace, and transient, and sure, so sure, of extinction? I don't mind that, but I'm also glad the soul congealed to flesh; I'm glad we're here, now.

Last class with Herr Jolles today. He said good-bye to me as I handed in the test of "Der Schmied"*—well, all over. German. They're bombing Hamburg now—April's getting closer—invasion month. Now in this April of our dying, God, grant us beauty and now dear God . . . and always . . . and give us also death, entire death.

---

*A poem by Ludwig Uhland about a blacksmith. Joan's teacher, O. J. Matthijs Jolles, was raised in Germany and left in 1934 due to his anti-Nazi views. He was asked to teach at the University of Chicago's Institute of Military Studies, created in April 1941, where he translated Carl von Clausewitz's *On War* to aid the war effort.

Sunday, March 9, 1941*

June 14, 1940—Paris taken
June 17, 1940—France surrenders
May 5, 1940—Norway gives up
May 13, 1940—Holland conquered
May 28, 1940—King Leopold gives up
June 10, 1940—Italy invades France
Oct. 15, 1940—First Conscription Day
March 9, 1941—Passage of Lend-Lease Bill (HR1776)

Sunday, March 16, 1941

Hullo. Well, here I am again, and cozy again too. Am lying in bed listening to *Tannhäuser*; have just finished *Of Human Bondage†* and some chicken broth. It took the hero [Philip] a long time to get his philosophy. I wonder if he got the right one: life is bearable because it is meaningless. Is it as simple as that? I wonder if I believe that. I truly don't know. I'd like to believe it, you know. Funny, I want mortality, too. What most people seem to dread, I want. . . . Good death after a sweet life.

I looked, as I stood in front of the mirror getting ready to go, at my full red lips for [a] moment. Then I wiped off the paint and my face was bare for a moment. I saw that the lips were not sensuous at all, that I had painted the sensuality on them. Underneath they were small and pale, almost

---

* Joan wrote the following dates and events in various inks on page 763 of her history textbook, which was Ferdinand Schevill's *A History of Europe from the Reformation to the Present Day* (NY: Harcourt, Brace and Company, 1940). This page concluded chapter 44, "Distracted Europe: Outstanding Factors of the Current International Chaos."
† A novel by W. Somerset Maugham.

ascetic. I saw suddenly that this was a symbol of what I was . . . what I had done to myself. I did not want worldly pleasures by nature, I had forced myself to desire them, like the paint I had put on my mouth, I had taken on the world . . . and it could be as easily shed . . . or could it? All this comes from reading realistic novels where a small thing can become a symbol for a whole life, a whole character. Emma Bovary's nails,[*] I'll never forget that.

We had quite a cozy evening at home. Mom was working[†] and came home late and ate in the kitchen. Daddy and I sat in the living room listening to Roosevelt practically declare war on Germany. I sat on the arm of Daddy's chair, one arm around him and one holding a glass of milk. I sipped it as we listened and offered him some. He shook his head but turned and bit my wrist gently. I ran my fingers through his hair. He said: "Doesn't this rouse your patriotism?" And I smiled and looked at him.

He's quite handsome really. I can't think of a boy I know who's as much my type. His fine sensitive, not sensuous, mouth and chin, his strong handsome nose, rugged brow, and deep, dark-lashed blue eyes. From his high forehead combed back the dark brown lustrous hair, graying over the temples. His figure is still splendid and slender. Mentally he is practically my type. And yet we have practically nothing to say to each other. We're not affectionate really, last evening was the

---

[*]Emma Bovary is the protagonist in Gustave Flaubert's novel *Madame Bovary.*

[†]It is not known where she worked, but there are several references to Joan's mother working during this spring and early summer. As a working-class family with a daughter in college, any extra money coming in would have helped, even with Joan's scholarship to the University of Chicago.

nearest to that in a long time. Is all human communication thus foredoomed to failure?

Tonight we ate chicken soup together during the *Ford [Sunday Evening] Hour** while Mom was in the living room. We spoke twice: once about the weather, once the music, cynically. You see how life is. Yet it's delightful. My father's fine face and noble brow might belong to a Roman, to a Viking, but anyhow, they belong to a *man*.

Monday, March 17, 1941

Ira said, "If you're wearing a girdle, it's a good one."

"But I'm not."

"Then," said Ira, smiling, "you're good."

Heard play *Cheers for Miss Bishop* tonight. A college life. . . . It's wonderful going to my school. I'm proud of it, of its ideas, of its cool democracy, of its dear honesty. It's good to go to a school you believe in. . . . Oh lovely, Gothic towers, filled with the spirit of our age! . . . If life is worth it because it is meaningless, you will not hide it from us. You will let us judge for ourselves—

And now to [wash] my sweaters.

Good Night.

P.S. Great blizzards in North Dakota.

Tuesday, March 18, 1941

Hullo. Germany is still poised on the brink of Greece and there are 100,000 British in Greece now and they're both trying to sign up Yugoslavia and Salonika is being bombed. Salonika . . . Oh! All the dream cities of the world are real.

---

*A Sunday-night music show on the radio.

Wednesday, March 19, 1941

Hullo . . . Betty and I saw *Gone with the Wind* today. Also had facials downtown. . . . Civilization's dead and dying. The world changed—our world too.

Friday, March 21, 1941

Sprig is cub. . . . I hab a slight cod id de dose as you cod see. . . . Mom's and Dad's wedding anniversary.

Guess who I went out with last night? You'd never. Leo . . . Father and I were sitting listening to the "China War Relief" program and I was knitting. We were recuperating from going out to dinner and the bookies as Mom was working. . . . The phone rang and it was Leo. I didn't want to go at first, but Father forbade me so I did. . . . Anyhow, I was still brooding over *Of Human Bondage* and didn't want Leo to think it was *that*. So—I went. . . . Went to BarBQ place on 37th, ate and drank tea and talked till about midnight. Then home. Exciting as you can see.

Went to the T.B. place yesterday. Dr. Freilich ordered another X-ray. (My right apex is still bothering him—whatever that is, just so long as it doesn't bother me.) So I went down to Washington Blvd. to have it made. . . . Lot of people in there—girls getting treatments. They've really got it. A thin blonde girl with beautiful hair and triangle face—just the type—and a glinting haired hussy with a gorgeous figure and the softest voice imaginable . . . others. Then I got my X-ray and left. . . . Must go to Dr. Freilich in two weeks.

Wednesday, March 26, 1941

Hullo, dear, you find me quite irritated . . . quite. First of all, the dear boy—Hugh, I mean—gets dramatic minded and lands for himself the male lead in *Yes, My Darling Daughter** which isn't bad—for him—but sure restricts his free hours . . . and he has to *kiss* Ruth Ahlquist.† And I must say he doesn't seem any too reluctant about it—though he doesn't know who the girl's to be yet. And then on top of that he has to get in the Collegium Musicum and play the flute—the flute!—in the rest of his spare time; and—on top of that!—his crazy roommate has to ask me to go and see the Northwestern Waa-mu‡ show with him Saturday night—his roommate! Oh! You see life is quite complex. I was quite open-mouthed when the roommate asked me—while Hugh was away for a minute and I couldn't quite get it through my head.

You know we're rather Platonic. Though I should have seen it coming. Even last night I was observing as I wrote in here that it was quite like a play in which you think you're in love with the wrong person. We're more congenial, you know. Always conversing. Only I *know* I'm not in love with him. It makes me rather sad about Iceberg§ too. It rather proves he doesn't like me, for I know his roommate wouldn't do anything to hurt him. I feel rather gloomy—or perhaps more irritated. Hugh didn't know about it evidently, for when he returned and I continued conversationally, "It was in the

---

*This was made into a movie in 1939 and a song in 1941; it was also a stage play.

†Joan's fellow student.

‡Annual musical revue show at Northwestern University.

§Joan's nickname for Hugh.

Tribune Sunday, wasn't it?" and so forth, Johnny* ignored me. They're quite an ignoring species. Hugh does it beautifully, too. They were discussing something enthusiastically, and when I broke in Hugh went on. Oh what a life.

I'm waiting now for Daddy to bring supper. Mom's working. . . . I got [a] C+ in German. Went in to see Mr. Jolles today. He was hidden by piles of work. He said I could easily have got a B if I had worked. I told him I worked harder in German than anything else. Which is true. Did I tell you I got [a] D in Social Studies—of all the easy subjects, it's humiliating!

Friday, March 28, 1941

C-Shop after a depressing session in Humanities. (We're studying the Treaty of Versailles. P.S. Yugoslavia has just revolted against joining the Axis and set up a new government. I suspect the British.)

Anyhow, C-Shop. Sat with Dougie and Betty and were discussing the farm when I saw Iceberg out the window. Kicked Betty and she began a discourse on how I should shave my legs more often. Then Dougie and I began speaking and Betty observed Iceberg and kicked me. I ignored her and she repeated—viciously. I continued talking to Dougie. Felt Iceberg appear. Stand for a minute, drag up a chair and sit down. Betty was kicking furiously. I'm black and blue. Finally I turned around and looked at him and Betty and I burst out laughing. Poor Hugh looked mildly surprised but we couldn't control it. . . . Finally he gave up and we recovered.

---

*Hugh's roommate.

Sunday, March 30, 1941

Hullo. Heard Hutchins today on the radio—spoke from Chapel. I meant to go and hear him but didn't arise early enough. He was good, he was wonderful. He was right. "The proposition is peace."* Probably most people won't agree with him—again. . . .

Wednesday, April 2, 1941

German measles. As you can see it was quite irritating. Lovely weather out and I felt fine but had to stay in and not read. Listened to all the crazy women's radio programs and washed my sweaters and hair. Went to Billings Hospital with my delightful mask Tuesday and the doctor laughed and sent me home. . . . Ho hum. Betty called me every night and told me school stuff. . . . It was terrible. My parents avoiding me and all the neighbors acting as though I was public menace No. 1. . . . And when Iceberg heard about my measles, he laughed—*laughed!* Incidentally, he can go to hell!

Well, anyhow I arrived at Student Health this morning, wonderful weather out—in my yellow silk blouse with daisy in my hair. . . . Anyhow, I had to wait and sat by Evelyn Steck who was coming *down* with the German measles and frightened and collapsed everybody. Especially when I told her about looking it up in our encyclopedia and me thinking it was the bubonic plague—only we don't have rats. Pierce Atwater across the way positively sputtered. She left and I said hello to him and then the doctor came and felt the bumps on my head and said I was alright. . . .

---

*Hutchins' speech is called "The Proposition Is Peace."

This was Good Friday. First time I haven't been to church since Grammar School. Was going to go tonight but Father asked me to go to the movies with him and Mom was working so I thought I could improve mankind better that way. We saw *Night Train to Munich*—British picture. Good but propaganda.* Home 11:30. Full moon, that's the full moon they're bombing Britain by tonight—and Berlin. Full moon—Good Friday. Fine for the bombers. . . . Father hurried to get home by 12 and I called him Cinderella.

Friday, April 18, 1941

Hullo, dear. If I did my homework half as regularly as I write in here, I'd be a brilliant girl. I have the potentialities anyhow. Life goes on, it was wonderful today—spring stepping up from the ground and the red poplar flowers sweet-smelling and damp. Finished hell week today and had mock initiation.† Betty and I ruined our beautiful song by singing it.

Iceberg came over while I was sitting outside of Humanities. I was considering cutting class but when he said he was going to cut too and would I sit out with him, I decided to go and discuss *Of Human Bondage*. Strange how the conscience hits us. But this wasn't conscience—this was perversity. He needs to be said "no" to now and then.

Later as I was sitting on the grass with my club sisters he came over and romantically recited the Greek alphabet to me. Also sang the Alma Mater. I had to learn them, you know. Then farewell.

Night Train to Munich stars Rex Harrison and Margaret Lockwood; it became one of my parents' favorite films.
†Initiation into the Wyvern Club.

Sunday, April 20, 1941

Hullo. Well, I got initiated today—into Wyvern Club . . . out at Irene Reynold's house. Lemnos, my pretty Athena's home, was captured this morning. Well, now to Descartes, Hume, Spengler and three pamphlets for Sosh. I'm rather behind as you can see.

Wednesday, April 23, 1941

Well, Greece is just about gone. King George II of Greece has retreated to Crete and at the same time bawls his army out for giving up. Consistent, eh? Churchill says, "There will be better times again," and the world is in a pretty state. Happy Birthday, Shakespeare. Sunday was Hitler's birthday. . . .

Annual peace strike at school today. They marched all 'round circle and ended up in Hutch Square.* Speakers and big crowd, mostly smirking and yelling against the speakers. I thought: hell, if they want war so much, let them have it. But I knew I didn't really mean it. Only I got irritated.

Time goes on. That bristle bearded Z— led singing afterward. Communist. Too bad, 'cause a lot of people can just be for peace who aren't for communism. I didn't have much moral courage today. I hope I'm not succumbing to convention—to my bourgeois environment at school. I should have got up and joined the peace strike, bought a poppy and proudly worn it. I agreed with them. I guess I haven't the moral courage. Well, I don't know. Maybe in a case where it mattered I would. Maybe you're happier if you don't have it. Maybe it's like joining a club. I knew what that was. . . .

---

*Presumably Hutchinson Commons.

P.S. Crowds are rioting as Col. [Charles Lindbergh] speaks for peace tonight in New York.*

Athens is fallen. So is Troy.

Thursday, April 24, 1941

Well, we sure have drifted—and I *do* mean apart. Hugh and I. Now we don't even sit together in the C-Shop—we scarcely talk.

Churchill's speech: Sat with the book open on my lap as he talked. Mom was listening too, and Daddy, cross-legged on his chair. "We shall not fail and we know we shall conquer or die." And Athens is fallen early this morning and the African battle is losing. But "we shall not fail."

He feels there is hope and help from America, from the West. And you know I always think "pigface" when I hear him, but today he said again and again in sibilants that hissed across the Atlantic, "we shall not fail."

And afterwards, the book shut on my lap, I wondered what it was, what these people were, that they could say we shall conquer or die. And all [of a] sudden I thought of Jane Mowrer.† And suddenly I knew. She was the epitome of the English. Her sweet fearless face, she would not have pity for a coward, she would not have pity for herself. You know somehow I never liked her; she was somehow the representative of what I was opposed to: the ruling class, the English, the proud, unbending English. And yet you could die for her. I can see how a man would die for her. She was splendid. Anything she would do would be splendid. Her health, her face,

*In this speech he argued that the United States was unprepared to go to war.
†A girl who graduated with Joan in 1940 from U-High.

without makeup, somehow pure, somehow vital. She could be queen of England or of faeryland. I can see how a man would die for her where he wouldn't for a thousand other women, where he wouldn't for me. She was the preservation of the race, not the individual. You would want to live for a Betty Crawford, my friend, but you could die for Jane, and know the future would be safe. But Jane next to Quizzie* and Quizzie looks *painted*. And I like Quizzie better. But I can see the final vivacity in Jane, her dark wavy hair, her shining eyes, too. Maybe that's England too, demanding all, yet all-giving. Maybe that's why the English can say, "We conquer or die."

Maybe England shall go down. I was thinking of Cicero today as we heard Churchill. And how those brave words would sound when some schoolboy is translating them, a thousand years hence. Maybe England shall fall. I guess so. I don't know.

Wednesday, May 7, 1941

Hello, time marches on. Stimson, Secretary of Navy, wants us to send navy to save Britain. They tried to get me to sign a petition for convoys today. I didn't, but Mr. Goldschmidt did. Woman stopped me on street today as I was carrying *Mein Kampf* for Sosh and asked me if that's what they taught me at the U of C. I defended my school—though it hurt.

Lovely day out, all white clouds and feather-edge and blue-blue sky and sun in green trees and lilacs, sweet-scented, blooming in the bushes and in girls' hair. Lovely day. . . . I really think Iceberg is crazy now. I was rambling along to Cobb [Hall] this morning and met him as I usually do. A little ahead of me, he turned suddenly and began to race back to Cobb. I thought: Well, it's pretty bad. . . .

*Joan's nickname for her friend Helen Quisenberry.

186

Arrived at Cobb and went upstairs to return Hitler and Hume.* Was just dumping them into the slot and wondering where the dear boy had hidden, when I heard a voice, "Let me put it in the slot for you, little girl." And a bony hand reached over and grabbed Hume. I almost collapsed and began to giggle. What had he been running for? He seemed rather silly and expecting me to go into the library, but I turned around and departed to Sosh, leaving him still panting from his run, his Adam's apple wiggling up and down. Well, it was good for his health—his hump.

Friday, May 9, 1941

Hullo. Times goes on. [Three hundred] British planes bombed German cities today. Pretty terrific. All the lovely spring has left us and it's got cold. . . . Yesterday wet rain. I sold tags for refugee aid outside Eckhart in the morning drizzle. *Mein Kampf* and my German grammar inconsistently beside me. . . . "Buy a tag for refugee aid." I thought it was Greek war relief till I looked at one of the tags. . . .

Wednesday, May 14, 1941

Well, Hess fled Germany Monday and arrived in Scotland yesterday. Quite exciting; no one knows why, or won't tell. . . . I think it's a plot of the Germans myself.† But you never know—the personality is sometimes awful strong. . . . [A year

---

*David Hume, the 18th-century Scottish Enlightenment philosopher and historian.

†Rudolf Hess, third in line to power after Adolf Hitler and Hermann Göring, apparently flew without permission and against Hitler's orders to England to negotiate for peace between Germany and England. He spent the rest of his life in prison.

ago] the black headline of France falling. France fallen. . . . And now this spring and this news. Time *does* pass.

Also today the Senate voted to give the president two more "dictatorship" powers as the *Tribune* calls them—to control industry in this "national emergency." These last quotes are my own.

The sunny air comes after the rain, the sky was blue and white after heavy down pouring this morning. The light silk blouses of girls flashing gaily. Life, I suppose, will sometime end. . . .

Sunday, May 19, 1941

Hullo. Time goes on. . . . Nice and sunny out today and I studied International Politics. Rather rueful to read about the League of Nations written once so blithely now.*

Monday, May 20, 1941

Went to church Sunday. Guest rector who cried as he prayed for "the people of Great Britain in their hour of trial." And for "our American Navy against its enemies." Funny, as he prayed for the struggling island, for all the anger in me, still, melancholy came, and, kneeling, I found tears in my eyes because it seemed that a world, good or bad, was going. A world that was our world . . . a world now going. And my hat lowered over my eyes to hide the gleaming tears. Religion is, I suppose, emotional. . . .

Well, now, what is Roosevelt saying? Still about our South American "brothers."

---

*The League of Nations was established after World War I to help prevent future wars. In the aftermath of World War II a similar institution was established: the United Nations.

10:10 p.m. Hello again. Well, he just proclaimed a state of "extreme national emergency." Also, though, he promised and stated that we would send convoys and defend by force of arms the freedom of the seas, etc. . . . Well, it's pretty close. I suppose we knew all along.

Friday, May 30, 1941

Hello—well this has been a truly delightful Memorial Day. It's been raining wetly up till now and a wan sun is beginning to smile; but rain or shine, I see it not. I've been locked in my room all day with Plato (sounds risqué, doesn't it, but then you know *Plato*) and have so many terms rolling around in my head now it may well burst. I'm inclined to agree with Plato when he says the young should not be exposed to too much dialectic. Sounds like a disease, eh; well, it is.

Aside from Plato, I've been studying pretty well these last two days . . . in Divinity [Library] too! I feel there's less distraction there, which is no lie. It's rather pleasant there too. These last days have been so hot and to sit in the cool, high-ceiling room with the wooden painted angels on the rafters and the heavy curtains blowing with the hot wind is quite pleasant. The floor is tile and, looking out the narrow, many-paned open windows at the exotic-looking locust trees outside, one can almost imagine he is in Egypt, or some such faraway place. The trees, with their tiny leaves on the long fronds might indeed grow under the sea, they are so foreign in appearance. The blue sky, the grey stone and the green trees, it makes a pretty picture as one looks out. Indeed, it might be a panel on the wall. As you can see, even in Divinity Library I get distracted.

Well, comps are coming. The Germans have practically finished capturing Crete which must shake the English faith a little. Crete was an island too, you know. They say Max Schmeling died trying to escape the English.* Memorial Day today—a lot to remember, a lot to forget. . . . Back to Plato.

Saturday, May 31, 1941

Went to Billings this morning [to volunteer] and, as they had measles, they sent me downstairs to read *Captain Horatio Hornblower* to a boy. Turned out to be Joe Harmon whom Emily was telling me about Wednesday . . . 19-year-old freshman from Purdue. Leg amputated just last week. Hurt it playing basketball. Nice-looking boy with good lean features, bright blue eyes and dark hair. I didn't read at all, we just talked—about college and everything. . . .

And all the sudden leaning there on the bed—he was telling me how he felt at first and I thought my god, he's got one leg cut off—oh poor boy—how terrible!—but I couldn't let him see I was thinking it. . . .

Somehow then the scene from *All Quiet on the Western Front* came back to my mind—where the two soldiers visit their friend whose legs have just been cut off and they realize how helpless they are—and I had that same feeling. So

---

*This rumor proved false; the renowned boxer lived to 2005.

I smiled foolishly and we went on talking about college and baseball. . . . And I think perhaps he was fooling *me*, too, talking about such trivial things—when there was a consciousness of something else there. . . . A nice-looking boy I might play bridge with in the C-Shop or meet on a double date. People, all round the world.

But he said, "I'm not going to let this thing get me down." I felt so moved in front of so much reality. After a while Emily came for me and we laughed that we hadn't been reading at all. Well, Joe Harmon, good luck to you. . . .

Time goes on. As I rode home I thought of that phrase of Francis Bacon's in his utopia*—used of the Governor, "He had a look as if he pitied men," and I think that is the most beautiful trait of all—"a look as if he pitied men."

Sunday, June 1, 1941

Well, come June, here it is again. I've been to the movies with Betty. We saw *Missing 10 Days* spy picture . . . and *Cheers for Miss Bishop* about university girl and teacher. Funny, but it made me cry—tears rolling down my cheeks. Made me think of my school years . . . my first college year . . . how I cried once in Freshman Week. Bud and I standing on the balcony with our arms around each other, singing "Auld Lang Syne" with my eyes shining wet, looking down at the circle of people we were to know, far below on the dance floor.

Somehow that first faraway day, I seemed to see the end before the beginning began. . . . I seemed to see us all old while we were still young. I seemed to see us all parting before we had met. That first faraway day. Singing "Auld Lang Syne." . . . And I could see myself looking back, like Miss

---

*Francis Bacon, who died in 1626, wrote of a utopia in *New Atlantis*.

Bishop after 50 years on that first 50th anniversary year of my school. . . . Looking back on Freshman week, that first crazy day on the streetcar with all the suitcases. . . . Walking home on a summer night with Dik, holding hands, entwined fingers. . . . The great dark shadows moving on the walk before us . . . and the poplars whispering above. . . .

An October night and Larry with strong arms around me and lips hard on my mouth, saying, "You deserved this," on the windy, star-spangled roof with the [Lindbergh Beacon] flashing by us. . . . Kaleidoscope a white-dark moment. Later downstairs, dancing silently together—bodies close together, yet we two with a stonewall raised between us. . . . And again later that night—the wreck, that crazy climax to a crazy night. Larry putting the fender in the car and laughing and saying, "This is fun, isn't it?" and I, still startled, agreeing.

All the days gone by: . . . a chilly sparkling winter's day and I with my fluffy bangs staring shining-eyed across the world at Larry, half rising with his eyes turned grey and boring into me. And the world dropping away around us; tiny biting bits of snow outside and crackling fire somewhere in our consciousness. . . . The night Bert came here with Larry and I wanted to die or burst or laugh. . . . The funny old days gone by. . . . "Should auld acquaintance be forgot."

Hugh and I walking home in frosty snow-flaked February night—almost zero out. Hugh and I sitting melancholy in U.T.* sipping red wine and bourbon and listening to a ghostly wind too close outside the door. Hugh and I play bridge: "You've trumped my ace again!" "Oh, I'm sorry, I always do." "S'all right." "Will we make it?" "No, but let's take a chance." "Was *that* your ace, I've trumped it again."

---

*University Theater, University of Chicago.

"Well, it's only a game." "How did I know you wanted me to lead a heart?" "Are you angry?" How many times did we play bridge together? We were always partners too. Sitting gloomy on the red leather cushions in Hanley's, spilled wine on my shirt, "The Last Time I Saw Paris" tinkling somewhere and "Rumania Taken" in black headlines a million miles away. All the funny days gone—my measles, damn them.

And now the end of the year, I guess that's a year you don't get back again. I guess you never get any back, not even a minute, not a split second, of all the past. But if you've had it, in another way it's yours. Spilt salt once too, that we forgot to throw over our shoulders, maybe that brought us bad luck too—or will. Well, good for the rich past, good for the present, and hail forever to the future, to the glorious, never-attained future. This was life, this was living—and now, Good Night.

Friday, June 6, 1941
Willkie has just spoken on the radio from Chicago Stadium—for unity behind the president—in wartime—ha!

Looks like French and British will be fighting each other in Syria soon.

Sunday, June 8, 1941
Hello. . . . Well, the British are fighting the French in Syria now. We knew it would happen. . . . Stayed in bed all day today and read Sosh. Delightful. Almost fell asleep with Hobbes. . . . The dear man is so boring . . . and population problems—ugh! I never could divide right. Well, it's all over Tuesday. . . .

It's pretty sad. . . . Tomorrow's really the last day of school. Next day I have a comp and then that's all. . . . I guess I'll go to graduation Wednesday. Life's purty sad now. I feel quite unhappy about it, though I suppose I'll be glad it's over too. . . .

Went to IF Sing* last night and only guess who won the quality cup! Hugh's fraternity—Beta Theta Pi—of all things—and they didn't sing well at all. I almost died at the announcement and so I'm sure did Hugh. . . . Saw Hutch[ins]! It was quite pretty. Red and white lights and lanterns hung all round the circle and high above in the black trees the biggest lantern of all, a full white moon, hung trembling in a clouded black sky. It almost rained but just didn't. We had quite good seats. On the grass at the top of the circle I wore my gypsy skirt and white blouse.

Quite jolly as you can see—my feet were killing me.

Time goes on—now back to Hobbes and *The Leviathan.* Fear I shall fall asleep again.

Friday, June 13, 1941

Hullo—Friday the 13th—Fine time to start writing in here, after a week. School's out as you may have guessed—a surprise! I'm working. Burry Biscuit Co. Factory girl after a year of college—father almost died laughing and forbade me to go but I went anyhow. He brought wine home for me tonight,

*Interfraternity Sing at the University of Chicago.

etc. . . . I'm gonna get paid $6 a week. He almost died again. Of course momma doesn't disapprove—she wouldn't! It's only for two weeks though—till I go to camp, so it's really nothing to get excited about. [Thirty-three cents] an hour.

I worked today already. Everyone was so nice yesterday when I went to look for the job. Helpful young men all over and old ones pointing out the way and all. When I got to this place a young fellow out back said I looked lost and escorted me in to the office. Today I ran into him again and he had to show me where the lunchroom was. He was standing among a whole lot of flour sacks. I thought he was an office boy! He came around later this afternoon—and, lo and behold, he isn't only the Big Boss, but he owns the factory. Oh joy, Joan, you're doing fine!

Anyhow, it wasn't bad today. It sure wasn't intellectual and I got the hang of searing the boxes (and not my hands) in about half an hour and had the rest of the morning to think. Once though someone came in looking like Larry and I seared my hands and forgot to breathe. I'd been searing my hands all the time though, so it didn't really mean a thing. It's not bad at all, really—I didn't like packing crackers so much though, 'cause you're in too much of a hurry, but you get used to it, I guess.

It's fun talking to all the girls and everything—I feel like Susan Lenox* or something—and where is it? Clearing, Illinois! Miles out and cows all around. What I like best is the walk over the dirt road from the streetcar. Green grass all

---

*A Greta Garbo film from 1931; the heroine becomes a woman of easy virtue. There is also a call slip from the university library tucked into Joan's *Graded German Reader* from October 1940 for the book *Susan Lenox* by David Phillips.

around and daisies springing up and *cows*—positively cows. It's quite delightful: Well—it's only two weeks to go, so why get excited? Mr. Davey* or Dean Smith should see me now—after all my Humanities! Ha ha—

Got my German grade—C. Purty good, huh? Hitler should know; I almost died.

Monday, June 16, 1941

Well—work today. Joan, the little factory girl. Only I wasn't today—Inspector Wehlen, call me. I inspected millions of army ration cans—for the USA. Defensive work. Caught myself humming the "Star-Spangled Banner" and reflected it was the same as making munitions. It is too, you know. Boss came over and worked with me for a while. We two alone all at the end of the belt. Only trouble was, I couldn't hear a word he was saying.

It's funny. It's rather mindless work there you know—as indeed I remarked to the boss. So as I get rather bored, I recite to myself or sing. Have gone through Housman†—Shakespeare—all the speeches from *Julius Caesar* and everything I like . . . the sonnets . . . "No longer mourn for me when I am dead."‡ It's really not bad. I fear in two weeks I may run out though—my repertory is not so large. The machinists there may have a strike.

Wednesday, June 18, 1941

Well, guess who's had quadruplets—not *one* baby—oh no, he couldn't do that—four he had to have! Who? My Eddie. Eddie

---

*Professor John R. Davey, who taught humanities for many years.
†A. E. Housman was Joan's favorite poet.
‡From Sonnet 71.

Adams! I went to camp counselor meeting at St. Chrysostom's and strangely enough was thinking about him as I walked there—you know I met him at one. Anyhow later at the meeting Norma told me. I began to laugh, I couldn't believe it—it seemed so funny. A hundred pound wife too—he always did like them small, said Norma, looking at me. Just think, they might have been yours, she added and I stopped laughing.

I'm to get $50 for the summer. From the looks of the future male counselors, I don't think I'll waste any money on summer clothes. Hmm—horrid!

Work goes on. Back on the army order today inspecting. They sent for me too. Boss fixed up a comfy corner for me and turned on the fan and brought me sugar cubes. Not very sympathetic as to my broken nail. Nice though: I can't get over the feeling I'm there studying the girls—and not really proletariat. It's quite irritating. I feel in league with the boss. My hands are all cut.

Friday, June 20, 1941

Hello. Time's a-passing. Still at the factory. Was going to quit today, but we get time and a half, 50¢ an hour for tomorrow. So am staying on. Passed 67,438 cans of army rations today. Uncle Sam doesn't know what I'm doing for him. Almost passed out today. Terribly hot. Ate salt tablet. . . .

Got first paycheck yesterday. [Forty-four cents]—for six hours and deducted for my uniform. [Two cents] on my Social Security. My old age is assured. Found a note from one of the girls in a can . . . I let it go. It was harmless and who knows when it may be found. In war, in blood, in pain. . . . Have begun singing the "La Marseillaise" instead of "Star-Spangled Banner" as I work. You can see how I've changed. Am dead tired. Oh my back!

Roosevelt's demanding reparations from Germany for *Robin Moor*.* Also consulates closed on both sides now. Well, they won't have my help after tomorrow. This is practically making munitions like I always said I'd probably end up. The cookies are hard enuf. I see the cans in my dreams passing before me in shining rows, like Charlie Chaplin in *Modern Times.* . . . Boss's name is Dan.

Friday, June 27, 1941

Got my permanent, etc., this week. My paycheck, incidentally, was $16.77. Sounds pretty good, huh? I wanted to frame it. [Seventeen cents] off on my Social Security. That makes me feel better. Who knows how I'll be when I'm 60.

Russia and Germany have been at war for almost a week now. Sunday morning Germany declared war. Sweden's letting (?) Nazi troops cross over her and Britain's warning her. It may not be long now. God help my poor grandmother and all the people there. Nils-Erik† would be in the army. I must write to my grandmother.

Well, I'm not going to keep up my journal this summer. Not enuf privacy at camp. Unless something exciting happens, of course. So I won't be seeing you for two months. "Bye Now."

Saturday, August 30, 1941

"Well, Joan," said Jim, taking my hand at the end of the summer, "they say the best of friends must part."

---

*A ship sunk by a German U-boat in May 1941 after the Germans evacuated it of its crew and passengers.
†Her Swedish uncle. Joan's paternal grandmother and all of the family on Joan's father's side (except for her father and one of her uncles) stayed in Sweden.

"I guess that's the truth," I answered. And it was. Summer was gone and good-byes were in order and most of us would never meet again. Jim Hogan, his good-humored Irish face, leaning against a wall and the sun shining hot from a bright blue sky and the kids all ready to leave. Looking up the road for the bus to come and seeing beyond the dull gold dust of the road the trembling shiny green cornfields and the dim hills beyond. Good-bye, end of summer, come again. Every year, the good-byes are sad and this year, I had for a while looked forward to the end of camp, but now it was really come, it was quite sad. . . . Now it was over and for a moment we could look back sadly on the faces we would not see again and clasp our hands again in an imaginary "Auld Lang Syne."

The first month at camp wasn't so bad. Of course, it was much stricter this year. We arrived on a Saturday and Tuesday night I committed my first sin—went to town in a canoe with Bob Mowrer and was given one 9:30 night out of three. That was only the beginning. The next week Norma and I went driving (it was a full red moon over the fields) to Niles [Michigan]. For four days we were about to be sent home and then they assigned us a second 9:30 night and forgave us. It was quite unpleasant as you can imagine.

I haven't told you about Burman yet 'cause I didn't know where to begin. At first, I didn't think of him at all. You know Norma had picked him out back in the city so I just thought of him as hers. But there was no one else and he was the best one there and Norma wasn't getting him, so we struck up a friendly rivalry. He used to come in the nature hut and play honeymoon bridge with me and the kids would tease and once we took the Brownies on a hike to the old mine and a mouse jumped out and I jumped into his arms but that was all for a while.

Then, one day, the last Tuesday of camp, we had a terrific thunderstorm, like a hurricane really, and he and I and Curtis McCrae were marooned in the nature hut. I have never seen a day when it seemed so much like the end of the world. Sky all purple and silver and the young sumacs bent to the wet ground by the wind. . . .

Next day we hiked the Brownies up to the schoolhouse and he asked me canoeing. All this time I had wanted him, you know, had been trying to get him—you might call this the first stage.

After canoeing—it was my 9:30 night—we went up the back stairs behind the library. Looking into the lighted room, we could see two boys playing ping-pong. We were only a wall away from them. He leaned back panting from our climb. I forgot to tell you we spilled into a mud bank by Sandy Beach on our canoeing expedition. Then he put his arm around me and kissed me. And then again and again. It was my 9:30 night . . . the bells began ringing. We got up and walked slowly back, the black trees swaying above us. . . .

The next night the kids had a moonlight dip, so we went to the Point. The fire was still glowing and we sat overlooking the lake and the silver-black water gleamed far beneath us. As he kissed me, I could see Vega, right over his ear, looking sedately down and for once I was angry at her complacency. Of course, she knows the world will come to an end!

The next night was Friday and his birthday and we took our night off and went into Niles. Walked out of one show and went and sat in somebody's backyard by the river. This time, mind you, since I had got him, I didn't want him so much; now it's got worse again. I get used to him and I miss him.

Then Saturday we went down again to the point and then came the last day Sunday.

The counselors were giving a party in the library and I had permission to stay out late and we went down to the point and built a huge campfire and moved a log so we could look over the lake. It was like the first campfire there ever was . . . and a man and woman. Night all full of soft sounds of insects about us. The moon, a new one, like a bent feather in the sky and a spangled reflection of her lying in the river. The soft hot wind. . . . It was the last night.

Finally we went back and joined the party. They began singing in there. Soft old songs, "Love's Old Sweet Song," "Auld Lang Syne," "Missouri Waltz" and then they began "Smile the While"* and I grew suddenly cold for a moment.

We walked home and bid good night . . . and good-bye then, for we knew morning would be too busy. I had on my sheer peasant blouse and a blue flower dirndl skirt.

Burman wrote to me. He came out to see me that first Monday and Mrs. P. wouldn't let him stay but she let me take that day for my night off and we went to Berrien that night. Movie—ate . . . necked in a pretty fir tree's shadow. The half moon was up. 11:30. She came in for me with a carload of counselors who made life miserable for me by singing.

As yet, I'm still in a pleasant state. I like him, but he likes me more and I still have to be pursued, which makes it nice for me. This is about the first time I haven't thought for once it's the real thing—(so I suppose it would be!) and I still feel that way about it. I don't expect or seem to want it to last forever, but I enjoy it now. Makes life quite pleasant. But why see too much of him and get us both tired. You can see

---

*From the film *Till We Meet Again*.

how mathematical I am. It's not like this when I'm with him though. . . . But I come out alright.

Oh, and then tonight. A Wyvern meeting was called rather suddenly at International House—and so went I. Nice to see my dear sisters again. Discussed rushing. Afterwards down in the garden for cakes and who should I see as I come tripping merrily over the flagstones who—but . . . well, I guess I almost knew when I heard Betty gurgle warningly. Of course who—Larry! I looked straight up over the white jackets (he's a waiter there now) into what I knew would be a pair of brown-grey mocking eyes. Luckily, we reached a table and I tumbled down and Betty chortled delightfully and my club sisters gaped.

That's all though. I sure know I'm not in love with him and never was. To think one little kiss could have caused all that commo-emo-tion. Though it didn't seem little at the time, to be sure. Anyhow, I just acted nervous from force of habit, I guess.

And, when we left, he had to ask were those all the little "*Weaverns.*" I don't know why, but it occurred to me afterward, why don't Burman and I go there Friday night, mebbe see a foreign movie or such? It would be fun. Of course that has nothing to do with Larry.

Monday, September 8, 1941

Roosevelt to speak tomorrow. "Important," they say. It was to have been Tuesday but on account of his mother's death they put it off. They say he'll say, "Shoot without being fired upon"—to our ships. I dunno. Well, we shall all die; somewhere over the far hills death is already written for such as us. I am young, but an ancestress of mine may have died younger. . . .

The years pass as surely as the days. Well, they are good and when it is all over you may not wish you had them back. We all have only so much sorrow, only so much joy. . . . Have been reading Emerson.

Friday, October 3, 1941

Went to movie tonight with Father. Saw *White Woman*—gruesome 1933 film. Did we really wear dresses *that long*? During the newsreel, half the people clapped and the other half hissed for Russia. I get a bit mixed up myself.

Friday, October 10, 1941

Hello, well, I should be speaking French to you after a week of that delightful language, but unfortunately (or fortunately) all we're having is pronunciation. Lord help us all. It's fun—though—I like all my classes—fairly well though I get rather bored in MVC* although it's an intermediate course.

Phy Sci† turns out to be rather unboring so far but I fear I am no genius in math. We have Dean Smith and he's just swell, you know, but I just *don't know* square root!

Germans say Russia is conquered‡ and they appear to be getting on to Moscow.

---

*Methods, Values, and Concepts.
†Physical science.
‡Hitler told Germans on October 3, 1941, that the Russians were vitually defeated.

Daddy and I went to see *The Way of All Flesh** last night. Not with Emil Jannings—though I saw that years ago—almost my first movie, I guess. That scene in the snow at the end, I remember.

Hugh's not back. *Es tut mir leid* [I'm sorry], I would like to have seen him again. I can't get over it, in fact.

Ran into former Sosh practice teacher today and all was as I and Betty had surmised. He said Mr. Goldschmidt said to him, "Remember those two girls who used to sit in the back and talk (and knit). Well, one got an A! I can't understand it." That was me—with the A, I mean.

Sunday, October 12, 1941

It's Sunday night now and we've just heard *Tannhäuser*, that's a beautiful thing, "The Evening Star." I always connect it with Algebra and Burton humming it during theorems—it's a pretty song. Mars is the evening star now. . . . Russia appears to be in a fix.

Well, it still goes on about Burman. I woke up this morning before anyone else and lay in bed thinking. I guess one can fall out of love as easily as in. Easier for me. Took less time anyway. I don't know 'xactly when it happened. Not where. I saw him, I think—before. Maybe that C-man smiling decided me but it must have started before. It just happens, I guess. What's the use of anything if it can go so quickly? I don't, you know, hate him or anything—I still like him, but it's not the same. Funny how that happened. I guess there's nothing you can do. Oh, I may still see him; he's supposed to come up here on the seventh [of] November and I may even go up there for a dance, but it changes, it does.

---

*The 1940 film, not based on Samuel Butler's novel of the same name.

Monday, October 13, 1941

Blue Monday, it rained, etc. *Maroon* meeting, class at hospital. To Cobb [Library] in the downpour to study. All the sudden, I looked up and everyone was looking up. It had cleared, suddenly miraculously, a brilliant sky lay before us purple and blue and all lovely colors. The green leaves hung on the trees alight with diamond raindrops and the yellow and red elm leaves burnt into the eyes. The very grey stone of the buildings seemed alive with color. And all this we saw through the rain-sequined windowpanes of Cobb. Beauty just about kills you sometimes. Then I went back to my Phy Sci problems.

Wednesday, October 15, 1941

Time marches on—and I hope ahead. Incidentally, so are the Germans. [Sixty-three] miles from Moscow and the snow is falling on the metal tanks. Brrrr.

Thursday, October 16, 1941

Betty and I were working in my notebook from last year and read over the little scribbling from those first freshman days. We almost wept, we were laughing and weeping at once over those days gone forever, saved only in the marginal notes during a Humanities lecture, a Sosh discussion. Oh, the past is even now fleeting, even now the present is become past.

Worked in *Maroon* office today writing headlines till seven with Bob Reynolds. I'm in love again, but I don't think this is serious. He let me out and we walked in to that quiet leaf-strewn street as the seven o'clock chimes were ringing, our footsteps soft on the pavement. He had a cold, he's beautiful.

Oh well now, I must do my French, gosh darn it.

Sunday, October 19, 1941

I went up to St. Peter's yesterday and sat up in front looking at the old faces and sights and all. Saw Eddie—he came up and took my hand and looked at me in the peculiar way he always had . . . time a past. And then Bob Barnes is married, since I've been there. I went out with him last Christmas—to the Christmas party and caroling in the shiny snow, remember? And I wouldn't kiss him. My gosh, time does pass, doesn't it?

And yesterday, Wyvern had a rummage sale on Lake Park—I worked there from two o'clock on . . . and almost went mad. But it was interesting. Lots of nice people—one who bought an evening dress just "to have one pretty dress." And she must have been pretty once—pretty trustful eyes and Irish black hair and sweet smile as she told me about her five children. Only her teeth were almost all gone. Lots of people. One old lady who tried to help. But then one mustn't laugh at them—to understand one's story is to weep with pity. It is depressing, though stimulating.

And in the morning I worked at Billings [Hospital]. Poor Dorothy.* She can't see anymore and barely moves. All deformed, her body. But her hair grows and her fingernails and she is lying there alive. Poor Dorothy, life has passed her by . . . has passed her by.

I must read my MVC and go to bed. Last night Daddy and I went to the movies and howled at *The Great McGinty*.

---

*A friend of Joan's who was ill.

Saturday, October 25, 1941

Hullo. Went to Field Museum today—long time, no see. Browsed around the way I like to and then went upstairs to the Fossil room. You know they have a big case at one end with a reconstruction of the carboniferous era: Giant insects and ferns and horsetail and mosses that were like trees. [Two hundred fifty million] years ago. The faint green light fell upon the floor of that unreal jungle, the soft carpetty floor and I thought almost alone in the great room. What if time were nothing? This very spot might have been the scene of that forest. What if I could step across time like a line, like any other dimension? What if I were to step through that narrow pane of glass into that unspeakable world? It looked so beautiful, so full of life and yet I knew, looking at it, that I should start screaming if I found myself in such a world. No human white foot had ever pressed that carpeted jungle. Only the drifting insects lighted upon the strange plants there.

The room fascinated me. The world 250,000,000 years ago. What unspeakable time has gone by. It is very true that man is a social animal. Not all the beauty in the world would make up for no people.

Went downstairs again and saw the Magdalenian Maiden who always makes me aware of death.* (She was about 18, it says, when she died.) And my other remote ancestors—the cavemen—and then to Egyptian hall where a darling little boy made me forget these gloomy thoughts with his screams of joy—out among the dead mummies. . . .

———————————

*The Field Museum in Chicago has the almost complete skeletal remains of a successor to the Neanderthals, dating from roughly 15,000 years ago.

Last night Paw and I saw *Out of the Fog**—a tale of gentle people.

Thursday, November 13, 1941

Day before yesterday was Armistice Day, if you can call it that—1941 AD. If we live, we'll look back on these days and know, perhaps, either that they were not as important as we thought they were—or that they were much more important. God, in the heavens, look down on the world! Today they finally finished repealing the Neutrality Bill.† Arm our ships and send them into belligerent ports—drums beating louder now—we had a peace meeting at school day before yesterday—what the hell, what is Armistice? Time goes on.

Just think, I'll be 19 in a month, getting old, gramma! I got the highest mark in our last French test—*94*—but we have another tomorrow so woe be unto me—also highest in Poetry on Milton. I don't like him—and Mr. Bond had me read my paper aloud. I was quite embarrassed. Passed Math in Phy Sci too—with the lowest C. Was quite happy! Whee! We're on astronomy now. Nicest boy, Bill Knisely, sits next to me everyday, talks and all—blonde, tall. I have been sitting with Bill since last Friday.

Burman came in last Sunday morning and we went to the Field Museum and looked at the Cave Men, etc., in the basement, spooky place. I'm definitely not in love with him but we have fun together.

---

*A 1941 film about fishermen who are terrorized by a gangster.
†One of the bills of the 1930s that came from noninterventionist desires. With its repeal, the involvement of the United States in World War II was only a matter of days.

Tuesday, November 18, 1941

Incidentally Phy Sci is bettah now. We had movies on the moon today. Bill is very nice.

Tuesday, November 25, 1941

Went to Billings about my back and got prescription. Study French with Mr. Yerke (René) at 11 o'clock. He was in France when the war broke out and was in the American ambulance corps for a week till they found out he was only 18. He'll be 21 tomorrow. It hardly seems like almost three years since the war broke out.* But I guess it is. My oh my . . . René wanted me to go out either Saturday or Sunday but I couldn't, I said.

Burman came in Friday and called me up at 8:30 but we had school even after Thanksgiving (it was the 20th)† so I told him to come at one. We ate cold turkey and washed the dishes and necked in the living room and seemed to be having a good time. But I knew it wasn't the real thing. Hell! Went to movie *Bluebeard's Eighth Wife* and necked some more. It was pretty cold out. Got home—ate more cold turkey in the kitchen and then he left.

Oh, life is just toooo delightful. I wonder if I'll be at school next year.

Wednesday, November 26, 1941

I'm so good I can't get over it. I studied almost six hours today. I think that's the most I ever have. And it didn't hurt at all. That's what's so surprising. Well, it's about time. I must try it more often.

---

*Actually, it was two years and three months.
†Thanksgiving was the third Thursday in 1941.

Worked in *Maroon* for while. I'm Exchange Editor, ya know. . . .

Dimanche Sonntag, etc., le trente (30) Novembre

Hello. Note French heading please. I feel pretty literary, à la Jules Verne, etc. (How about a trip to the moon, confidentially?) I've just had milk on top of a Tom Collins,* which let me tell you is no way to preface the study of Phy Sci.

They played "Birmingham Jail" on the radio in the car. That's a sad song.

Tuesday, 2 decembre, 1941

Hello . . . getting colder out but then I suppose we were lucky to have it nice so far. Got an F—not just F but minus in French verb blanks. Delightful. Have to write each mistake right five times. I got writer's cramp.

During lunch hour Betty and I ate in Eckhart Hall and played with a big globe of the world that was like Charlie Chaplin in *The Great Dictator* . . . an old globe—Austro-Hungary, etc. It rolled heavily around on the floor while we danced about it.

P.S. Crisis with Japan, it seems.

Thursday, December 4, 1941

Remember that tall C-man? I met him again today—in elevator. He said, "Hello. I didn't recognize you at first." And then apologized for not saying hello some other time. I couldn't remember but forgave him. I don't know where he thinks he knows me from.

---

*A popular cocktail made with gin.

Friday, December 5, 1941

Hello. Brr—'tis bitter tonight. Blowing like a wind from Hades but still somehow a little like spring. Sort of fresh and dewy, you know, with all the force behind it. . . .

French this morning. René Yerke and I had a bet on the verb blanks, if he got a lower mark than I, he had to write all things wrong five times over for Mr. Rollard and visa versa for me. We were almost disappointed when we both turned up with A's.

Met Betty. We were laughing about how all week, every time I started into Phy Sci to meet my blonde at the back, some little voice would call me and I'd never get there. I swore no one was going to stop me today. Just then Gloria came along and we both burst out laughing. Poor Gloria. But she departed and I got over there without her and then, just as I was slipping into Phy Sci, I heard her little voice, "Joan." But I was determined and dragged her back with me and her friend too—some girl who had a comfy seat already. Then Bill came in and sat down next to me.

Stevenson was very good today—funny and all—he poured carbon dioxide (you couldn't see it) into a paper bag and it went down. It was spooky. Other experiments with gasses too. He's so careless. Yesterday he left a Bunsen Burner going. If he starts teaching Chemistry, I know he'll blow up the building. Can't you see him with nitro-glycerin. Anyway—don't mistake me though—he's very brilliant.

Anyhow, as we were leaving class, Bill asked me to go and see *Native Son*, a play downtown next Saturday and I blew away into the wind.

Sunday, December 7, 1941

Well, Baby, it's come, what we always knew would come, what we never quite believed in. And deathly calm all about it. No people in noisy excited little clusters on the streets. Only silent faces on the streetcars and laughing ones in windows. No excitement. Only it's come. I hardly knew it, never believed it. Was saying only today to Ruth as we sat by the fire in Palos Park that I would hate it—would never believe it. War with Japan. And other people there discussed, the way we used to discuss the "Road to Peace"*—as though we could turn it over and put it away and think about it again sometime. And last night as we went out, the radio told of the possibility and we said it was just another war scare. I guess it wasn't. I know now it wasn't.

Today Japan declared war on the United States. She bombed Pearl Harbor and the Philippines while her diplomats were talking peace to Roosevelt. This afternoon at 2:30. My God, we never knew! We were drying dishes out at Evelyn's place and I churned butter and went for the well water with Ruth like Jack and Jill. As I churned, I could see my image—in my red jerkin and light sweater and pearls in the mirrored curved face of the pots, in the kerosene lamp. Three images, all churning and I looked out at the peaceful frosted autumn hillside. "That time of year . . . when few or no leaves hang."† And the earth was turning and it had happened. The cheery rattle of the dishes and our laughter and the crackle of the fire. We went out to the pasture and brought back the

---

*FDR made a speech announcing the second New Deal on October 31, 1936. It ended with the words, "That is the road to peace."
†Joan's version of Shakespeare's Sonnet 73.

horses and saddled one and rode him in turns . . . till we froze and came in.

Right then most people knew. Not we. One of the fellows drove us into the city and then Ruthie and I took the streetcar and saw a bright headline. US and Japan near war. And waited in a quiet tavern for another streetcar and got on and gasped to see in black placid letters as though it had been said before: "Japan Attacks U.S. We are at War." And saw two Japanese on the streetcar, gravely watching us. Came home, discussed it excitedly through supper. Listened while they broke into programs on radio to give flashes.

But somehow, it had already happened. Somehow we were looking through a window at a future that had been written down a long time ago. God, God.

Betty called up and we were excited. . . . Japan has formally declared war on US and Britain. God, God, all the world is in this now. I'd much rather be at war with Germany than Japan. I like them better. . . . Funny logic. But I wouldn't be so afraid to have them win. God, what is there to be left of our world when it is all over? I guess it won't be the same. Or will it?

Tomorrow Roosevelt talks to Congress to declare war. Twelve o'clock. . . . The days are here, the days are coming. Oh God, God.

We never knew. We always knew.

Dutch East Indies and Costa Rica and Canada have already declared war on Japan. Us tomorrow.

Well now I must read my MVC methods. Methods, Values and Concepts. That's almost funny.

We listened to *Sherlock Holmes* and then Ruth left.

Last night we met Bill of all things and things weren't too friendly for a while. I met Kenny through him, you know. We went to Capitol to see *Citizen Kane* which I didn't understand, as the mental morons I was with made me leave in the middle. Who the heck was Rosebud? Then bowling at 1:30 and to Sam's for Tom Collins and then home—3:30 and read Phy Sci for an hour. It's amazing!

Monday, December 8, 1941

Well, the first day is over. It's unbelievably calm. Walking to school with Ginny Banning, discussing it and listened with great crowd in Reynolds Club at 1:30 to Roosevelt's declaration. England declared war at 8:30—beat us . . . my God—we are at war!

Tuesday, December 9, 1941

Now that the day has come, we are unbelievably calm. There are black headlines but no excited voices. One plays bridge and asks what is trump and repairs lipstick and reads Plato and John Keats. One reads the comic strips and the headlines eyes equally unmoved, face like the images of gods. . . . Not with excited bravery are we now, who always knew it was to come, never believed it would, but with a still acceptance that bids life go on. . . .

And yet today planes flew over San Francisco, planes with the Rising Sun upon their wings,* and ships were sunk and men were killed and blackout in New York. The quiet faces, the unbelievably quiet days. . . . Tonight walking home over the dark campus, I looked up and saw great Venus shining calmly and red Mars like an eye watching gravely. One red leaf rasped noisily over the cement caught in the wind, yellow

---

*Such rumors were common just after Pearl Harbor.

lights shone from the houses. The bells were ringing. The world was gently quiet. And yet the day had come.

"Thee, when death conquers us, others shall praise."

Heard Roosevelt tonight on the radio; he said we must be prepared for a long hard war.

Saw Purr* today—he says he's getting ready. Mr. Yerke says he's going to volunteer. And then tonight I went over to the store and as I walked along the quiet cold street, I was thinking about the draft—they're planning to extend the age limits. And all the sudden, I thought, "Burman will have to go." I hadn't thought of it before in connection with him. Oh my God—the world we half-dreamed of is here!

Wednesday, December 10, 1941

Hullo. Mr. Yerke won the bet on our French verb blanks today and I had to correct both of ours, writing each thing five times. But then I won yesterday.

The Jap paratroops have captured Luzon in the Philippines and sunk two British ships, the *Repulse* and another near Singapore. Hitler speaks to Reichstag tomorrow. We just heard the first casualty lists over the radio. Lots of boys from Michigan and Illinois. Oh my God!

Life goes on though. We read our books in the library and eat lunch, bridge, etc. Phy Sci and Calculus. Darn Descartes. Reading Walt Whitman now. Bill from Phy Sci came up to me after class when I was standing with Betty and asked my name. He looked quite embarrassed, poor boy. I told him and began prattling of Hugh and Betty laughed delightedly. Saw him again in Cobb this afternoon as I was doing my poetry. He came over and we went to Commons Room and talked for

---

*Bob Purrington.

an hour. . . . Later I went to the bookstore to get a card for my grandmother and who should I see before the stamp counter but *his* bright and shining face! I almost died.

Thursday, December 11, 1941

Well, the world is wheeling around, 24 hours a day, never ceasing, never pausing, never hesitating. We cannot relive the ecstatic moment, we cannot repeat joy, but life is just, neither must we repeat pain, suffer again what once was suffered. Only the world repeats itself. Today Germany has declared war on the United States. And Italy too, of course. Remember, I told you yesterday Hitler was to address the Reichstag today.

Well, he did. I was combing my hair this morning when they broke into a *Morning Melodies* program to tell us the news! Before I had grasped it the music switched back on. I walked in and told Mom. She said I was having delusions. They'd say more about it. But I was right. Ten minutes later the announcer told us all. Well, I guess we always knew. But we didn't think we'd be so calm about it. But it's really not exciting. Really, it has happened already. For us, it has happened already.

The light in the skies has gone out already. We were always Troy. It was a calm cold Sunday the day it happened. But, in our hearts, it had already happened. We knew we were born to die. . . . With the news in my head I walked to French and we read Victor Hugo. The world is so full of a number of things, I'm sure we should all be as happy as kings.* The world is so full of a number of stings, I'm sure we should all be unhappy as kings. . . .

MVC . . . Phy Sci . . . Matter and Force. Sat with Betty, not Bill. Lunch, read *Pulse* . . . Poetry. "Ode on a Grecian Urn." Fanny.† . . . Planes over Los Angeles yesterday. Studied. Went to Volunteers' tea. Worked in *Maroon* on Student Opinion cross country. I'm glad I go to a sane university. President Hutchins hasn't said anything yet. The time is growing short, the time is here. There is a tight cord under one's ribs. There is a tight throbbing under one's wrists. Soon no more throbbing, no more pain. Soon quietness, first death. Death is a kind mother. I would like to be the earth and hold you in my arms forever.

Man is beautiful, unspeakably beautiful. Man is committing suicide, cutting out his guts in an art museum, filled with lovely things. Man will see beauty as he dies.

The chilly *decembre* wind is blowing dead leaves across the street. Some day there will be a pile of dead leaves in a gutter. Lovely—and untouched.

Sunday, December 14, 1941

No fooling, Toots, I've been going to this school for more than a year and this is the first time I've gone out with the proletariat there. No fooling. I thought of it as I undressed tonight.

---

*"The world is so full of a number of things, / I'm sure we should all be as happy as kings" is a couplet by Robert Louis Stevenson entitled "Happy Thought." It appears in *A Child's Garden of Verse*.
†A poem by John Keats; Fanny was Keats's beloved.

No one of the others, Purr, Bud, Larry, Dik, Bert, Hugh, Johnny, oh never Hugh! None of them even approached the proletariat. Well, maybe approached, but never were. And my club sisters and the people I sit in the coffee shop with day after day. They really are shallow. I never quite realized it before, though I always knew, I guess . . . and I had a good time tonight. After all, I've got a few brains, but I'm always afraid to use them in the Coffee Shop, in the company of my friends. Unhappy thought, eh?

Anyhow—went to see *Native Son*—got home from Ruth's at a quarter to seven and Bill came at 7:40 and I had to bathe, dress and eat so you can imagine how relaxed I was.

We departed and walked to the UC with another couple. Somehow you never realize the brilliant people who go to the U—the ones who spend years in a Chem. Lab. and get Phi Kapp keys* and finally discover something wonderful, who never go to the Coffee Shop, really exist and have girls and friends and go to plays and drink, etc. Maybe you wonder who they do it with. Now I know.

Bill belongs to the Co-op on 54th and Ellis. Play was good. Social drama—significant, you know. Afterwards we took the bus to the Co-op, their house, and went in for social purposes. Bill's room, double-decker beds—real cute. There I go getting shallow again. We went downstairs and ate and drank Tom Collins and talked and smoked and listened to war news and music indiscriminately. Stayed till two o'clock. Then we left. Walked home, chilly and slippery out. Brrr. Home. G'night. Now to read the *Tribune*. Really, it's shocking,

---

*Phi Beta Kappa keys—the symbol of the honor society.

the insipid lot I go with. I always knew but never realized and shan't change now I fear, having *become* insipid myself.

P.S. We were in the midst of a red-light district in the play and I didn't understand and had to come out in a loud clear voice, "Where is he?" and then Bill *had* to explain. Oh me. Night!

Monday, December 15, 1941

Well, hello. Had my French comp. at night of all times—after, René and I decided to celebrate so we went to the movies, the Frolic, and celebrated calmly eating candy like children.

In *Lady Be Good*, they sang "The Last Time I Saw Paris,"* and through her face you could see the parks and the streets and the churches and the Eiffel Tower over all and I remembered last winter and Hugh and snow falling and "The Last Time I Saw Paris" in Hanley's and I thought of Bert, who saw Paris that last mad summer when the war was breaking out. "It wasn't exciting—Paris was declared an open city."†

Friday, December 19, 1941

Hello. Well, they've passed the bill for conscription of all men 20 to 45—registration of all 18 to 64. That includes purty near everyone. Daddy brought home wine tonight. I knitted and drank too much and am still slightly dopey from it with a pleasant unwillingness of my bones to do anything—as you can no doubt tell from my handwriting. My last night of 18— Remember last year? Poor Dale in the army air corps now.

---

*This song won the Oscar for Best Original Song in 1941.
†Bert's comment on December 7, 1940.

We never thought these things last year. Poor Philbrick. Last night I was studying my Phy Sci in the *Maroon* office and the *Chicago Sun* called up and asked for information about him. I gave it. Poor Dick.

Heard Hutchins speak today. Banning and I and Betty waited half an hour outside of Mandel Hall to hear him. He's wonderful. He came out all alone and spoke in front of that great red curtain and smiled and then went out while we were still clapping. [Two thousand] people there, *Tribune* says. . . . He's wonderful, he's God. . . . He says we should win the war now that we're in it. You know how he felt before: "The Proposition is Peace." Well, he changed his mind. I don't know what else he could say though.

It's different from last year at Christmas. Last year, they had candles in the C-Shop and played Xmas carols and everyone sang and was jolly. This year it was warm and springy out and bright sunlight in C-Shop and no singing. Some people half-heartedly tried.

Time goes on. Bill called up last night. We're going to the ballet New Year's Eve.

Tried studying with my club sisters for first time. Surprising how much easier it is to concentrate. Got B in poetry, may still get an A though. Mr. Bond said he enjoyed my work.

Tomorrow's my birthday. Father brought home a chicken.

Christmas and birthdays make you think of things. I'll be 19 tomorrow. We have tragic privilege as *Time* magazine observes of living in a world of crises. . . .

P.S. Paw and I talked Strindberg and Zola and Hearn,* etc., over our wine. Good talk and dying world.

Sunday Morning, December 21, 1941, 3:15 AM

Well, here I am healthy and hearty in spite of my old age of 19 and feeling like the living example of late hours bring on good health. I feel as if I could lick 20 Hercules, though I probably couldn't. Kenny and I were going to go out to Calumet City tonight so he arrived at eight after Paw and I had just had a birthday feast of chicken and the darlingest cake!—and wine. And he got me the cutest Baby Ben alarm clock!

Anyhow, Kenny arrived and we went to Jack's house and drove with Jack *et* mates to 63rd and drove around while they shopped and took mates back and Kenny and I went to his house and I met his mother and dad—she's much younger— both of them are—than I expected. Very nice and asked me to dinner sometime, etc. He tells me Ruth (his sister) approves of me too. He said he wanted me to meet his parents 'cause they say he never goes out with a nice girl. . . .

Anyhow then we went to pick up a girl for Jack to take her home and I got the shock of my life when they started to discuss Beverly Kennelly. They picked her up one night it seems. That's the way you hear familiar names again. Names in dark cars. And we used to take imaginary photos in

---

*August Strindberg was Joan's father's favorite writer. Likewise a dour Swede, Strindberg shocked readers with his graphic description of the war between the sexes. Émile Zola, a 19th-century French novelist, naturalistically showed the lives—often corrupt or debased—of all levels of society. Lafcadio Hearn grew up in Ireland and traveled to the United States. His most famous writings are about Japan, where he lived from 1890 until his death in 1904.

Ryerson Gardens!* Anyhow took girls home and then ate and then to Cal City. Beautiful drive. Stars all frosty and a-gleam and red fires of steel mills and we passed a train of tanks on the way back and a policeman or soldier at every bridge.† They wouldn't take me in any place out there—it must be purty bad—except the Siesta Club and we couldn't get a table there so we came back—all frosted night—to Zebra Lounge—drank—then to bowling. I did 64. I'm improving and then played shooting at submarines. I got 8,000, Jack 8,900, Kenny only 4,000. Washington should hear of this. Jack, too, is subject to draft now by the way. . . . Kenny got me a lipstick and Lucien Lelong Poker Chip cologne. Purty smell. . . . Just think—I'm 19 now. I feel old and sophisticated.

After teaching today went to bookstore to get stamps. Bill was quite flustered and gave me $1.25 change for a dollar. I gave it back. Me and Lincoln. Later he called up and asked me out for tonite, but I had a date already.

Friday, December 26, 1941

Well hullo, Xmas and all that stuff all over. I'm not as cynical as I sound, of course. But it's over. We lost Hong Kong, and Manila we declared an open city. Merry Christmas, Japan. Churchill is here and all comradely, etc., with FDR. Brotherly-love, et al. Pigface! Christmas night it rained pourpour and the skies weeping. I doubt that the gods really care though.

Tuesday night Daddy and I went out and bought a tree and decorated it all and surprised Mommy when she came home. Monday night I stayed home and finished Burman's

---

*Today known as Ryerson Woods, located northwest of Chicago.
†They were there for security purposes, in case of sabotage.

scarf and listened to Orson Welles give "The Happy Prince." It always makes me happy-sad. "Swallow-swallow, Little Swallow."* Last summer I almost went blind reading it in the bright sunlight around the flagpole to a group of kids. Afterward all I could see was yellow spots. But it is a lovely tale.

Anyhow, finished the scarf. Tuesday and Wednesday shopped. Gloves and scarf for Daddy—purse for Mom. Wednesday went to mail Burman's present to him; hadn't got his yet, but knew he was sending me one from his Xmas letter-card. And as I wrapt the present I thought: I never want to see him again. I didn't want even to send the scarf to him but then I'd been knitting on it so long for him it really seemed already his. And I thought of enclosing a card with "This is good-bye" on it, but it seemed overdramatic and not the thing for Xmas anyhow, so I didn't. Mailed it, but suddenly discovered I was completely through with him. Completely. Then I came home and got his present which didn't change my mind any.

Got Xmas card from Greek god†—remember how thrilled I once would have been. Didn't mean a thing. Eddie's joining, couldn't see him this afternoon either, though it was a lie. I just didn't want to see him. I wasn't too subtle. I said, "Well, drop me a line sometime," but I was as cold as "Birds' Eye string beans." Hung up and came back to my knitting for half-an-hour. Went down to visit Mom washing in basement. Funny how quickly, how easily, love dies. Of course, though, that wasn't love, but even so, quicker than the turn of the head or the wind in the trees or the cold snow melting, it dies.

---

*A line from Oscar Wilde's "The Happy Prince."
†Paul Kappe.

Sunday, December 28, 1941

Hullo. Merry Christmas or whatever it is. The Japs are bombing Manila. Declared an open city, you know. Well, I guess we never really had any delusions about dove-winged peace. . . . [A caroling party], lay under Xmas tree, looked at lights and listened to radio.

On way home began remembering that last caroling party and that moment when we sang "Auld Lang Syne" and Johnny's arm tightened and we were aware of time. And suddenly it was as if the past had never been, or rather as if the past were still the present. I thought of last year and suddenly I was looking right up into Larry's eyes the way I did that cold December day we met again. It was as if the moment were still there. All the moments. I guess the past is ours . . . forever . . . never. . . .

Reread my journal after listening to *Tristan and Isolde* after I got home. Am about to read John Donne now. Nice and comfy.

Is it natural or does the past always seem more exciting than the present? As I read over my last year's journal, it seems that something was always happening. . . .

1942

Age 19

"Let us at least die like ladies and gentlemen."

Thursday, January 1, 1942

Well, Happy New Year! Here it is, another date again—time is always passing, but it doesn't seem to go so dreadfully fast anymore. It's pouring out now. Heavy, long drops of rain and some hail too. Happy New Year! Hail and farewell.

Last night Bill and I went to the Ballet Russe. Saw Toumanova and Danilova. Best [dancers], you know. *Gaîté Parisienne*, *Scheherazade*, and *Magic Swan*. . . . Nice. Went back to the house for party, just got outside as the whistles began blowing. Happy New Year. . . . It had been snowing and was clear and cold. Party, drank, ate—toasted New Year. From far away I hear "Auld Lang Syne"—a sort of will-less nostalgia hit me. Home—about four o'clock. Mom thinks Bill looks like a Groton* man. She has her delusions. But then I liked him

---

*A private boarding school in Massachusetts.

before I went out with him. That's always the way with me. I mean, I still like him, but not as much. Lord, what'll I do when I'm married? Probably grow to hate the man!

Friday Afternoon, January 2, 1942, 4 PM
Manila has just fallen! Bye now!

Friday, January 9, 1942
Hello again. More than Manila has fallen. Principles are dropping too. I'm supposed to sell defense stamps even. Philippines appear to be a bit too warm, even to this chilled winter world. It's been below 0° all week here.

School's started again. Club meetings—C-Shop—bridge. Lenore Blackwood and Yvonne Martin took engagement rings. Dave got married. Must be the war. Went to lunch with René at the Hut today, as I had no money and was facing starvation. He's been asking me out for months and seemed a bit startled when I finally accepted. I ate plenty though and had to take a date with him for a week from Sunday. Some play we're going to see. Bill asked me out for tomorrow night Thursday, but I said I had a date. It doesn't hurt to say no now and then. Anyhow, it's so cold and he hasn't a car. I wonder what's happened to Kenny? He must be dead—or in Kentucky.

Sunday, January 11, 1942
Hello. We've just been listening to *Pirates of Penzance* on the radio. Jolly little operetta. Hard to believe we're at war. Now the Symphony. . . .

I simply must read Phy Sci, but it always makes me want to cry, I feel so dumb! I got B in it though. Also A in French and

C in MVC. I'm not so logical. Dunno about poetry yet. . . .
We're reading *Huck Finn* now in Fiction.

Baked lemon cream pie today, delicious and finished
Emily's mitten and started the other.

I simply must do my Phy Sci now.

P.S. Got a byline on my story in the *Maroon* Friday about
war preparation across the country in colleges.

Friday, January 16, 1942

Time goes on. I've resolved to study every day but you know
how often I've done that. Honestly tried to read [Jane Aus-
ten's] *Emma* this afternoon but found myself looking at the
wallpaper et cetera instead, so went to C-Shop and played
bridge.

School is getting rather man-less on account of draft, war,
etc. So . . . Betty asked Purr about his being engaged—or
rather told him—so he's being rather huffy. Kenny called
up—he's got ulcers. I laughed when he told me, but of course
it's really not funny. Quite painful, I understand.

Made a lemon-cream-pie Wednesday night and went to
Red Cross with Emily. Must read *Emma* now.

'Nite.

P.S. Got [an] A in Poetry and finished Emily's mittens.
Bob Lawson looks like the Lost Generation. Sort of seedy,
but you can just see him in a uniform, dying splendidly for his
country—anywhere.

Sunday, January 18, 1942

Well, it's like old Mr. So-and-So used to say: "You pays your
money and you takes your choice." Either you go out with
people you like and spend the evening trying to make an

impression on them—or you go out with people who like you and they spend the evening trying to make an impression on you—and you get bored. It's rather awful really, nobody gets satisfied. And I always feel sorry for them, too, and wish I could kiss them good-night and so make them happy. But I can't be a liar. Of course sometimes you go out like Burman and me. Neither of us was trying to make an impression. We were both only concerned with getting what we wanted and we both got it—and as far as I can see—no one was hurt. That's more sense to it, as I see.

Anyhow—went out with René Yerke tonite and *he* belongs to the second class—which brought all this on. We saw *Pal Joey*, a play at the Grand Opera House. Quite dirty, but for all its gaudiness rather sad, as all the critics remark, because it holds up to such illumination the cheap side of our time, which is in a way the cheap side of man. All people concerned with getting what they want. Yet in a way, likeable.

However, as to feeling sorry for the second class, as Moll Flanders,* whom I am now reading, says—no matter how you pity a man before, once you yield to him, he no longer pursues you, and you are the one to be pitied, which seems, sadly enuf, to put man and woman forever on fighting terms.

Tuesday, January 20, 1942

Heard Stephen Vincent Benét† tonight on "Poetry and History." He was remarkable. Clear yet forceful. He appears to think we can come out of the war thumbs up. . . .

---

*The protagonist of Daniel Defoe's novel who gets married numerous times, including to her own brother.
†A Pulitzer Prize–winning author.

1942

Mr. Benét was talking about diaries in history and I believe I have written mine with the intention of having it read some-day. As a help, not only to the understanding of my time—but to the understanding of the individual—not as me—but as character development. Things we forget when we grow older are written here to remind us. A help not only in history but in psychology (I can't even spell it). If I can do that, I believe I shall have done all that I could wish to. I rather like the idea of a social archeologist pawing over my relics.

'Nite.

Thursday, January 22, 1942

Hello. Lost Generation nothing—huh! More like Lost Delu-sions. . . . I've just been nite-editing with Bob Lawson. Oh—men, a-men—ah men! It was nice and balmy out and we drove through Washington Park and they played "Blue-birds Over the White Cliffs of Dover,"* etc. Oh men. They're all alike. But one can forgive them when you think in a few months they may be dead or about to die. Poor Bob Lawson who wanted to be a writer. I can see his tombstone—but they won't have those—now. . . . Gloomy, aren't I? I forgive him. This depresses me.

Anyhow, time goes on. Took Red Cross course last nite again. Learned how to bandage. Cakes with Emily afterward. Today sat for 1½ hours with a white veil over my head collect-ing money for Red Cross. Boy in my fiction class who always argues with me went by and said I was succumbing to hys-teria and that I looked very cute but gave me a contribution anyhow.

---

*"(There'll Be Bluebirds Over) the White Cliffs of Dover" became an iconic song of World War II, immortalized by singer Vera Lynn.

Now it's almost two, but I don't feel at all sleepy. I should read MVC but I donwanna. Funny, as we were getting out of the car to go into empty Lexington about one o'clock tonite my book fell and I said, "Oops—there goes Moral Values"— and Bob laffed and laffed. But *that* was the name of the book!

I like the people down at the printers. Steve remembered me and called me Joan though I've only been down a very few times (four in all) and the girl did and all. They always make me feel jolly.

Late January 1942*

Kant:† "Morality is a matter of being as intelligent as possible in a concrete situation." Purty good.

Sunday, January 25, 1942

Hello. We're listening to *H.M.S. Pinafore*, etc., now on radio. Nice and jolly.

I baked a cherry pie today. "Can she bake a cherry pie, Billy boy, Billy boy?" And it was luscious!

But I was suffering with a wisdom tooth (my first) and so could not fully enjoy it.

Bill called up and wanted to go out today but I didn't. He's taking a full-time job now out at South Chicago and taking Phy Sci nights at school now. We're going to the basketball game Saturday night.

They're going to start rationing sugar next month. . . . We never would have believed it. Mom looks quite Boushwa‡ in the living room, knitting for the Red Cross and listening to

---

*This entry came from Joan's school notebook.
†Immanuel Kant, famous German philosopher.
‡Joan's attempt to spell *bourgeois*.

"Stay close to your desk,"* etc., from *H.M.S. Pinafore*. The world may be a lot changed—so changed that Gilbert and Sullivan may someday bring tears to our eyes—for a world that is past. . . .

Hutch has decided to give the BA in two years—sad, but too late for me.

They played "Auld Lang Syne" on the radio tonite and it was as if one could already see the world from one's grave. And the past was forever past. Just as that first sweet Freshman week when I cried that we must all part.

Thursday, January 29, 1942

P.S. Rearrangement in *Maroon* staff. I am now Asst. Office Manager of both Editorial and Business Offices. Some fun, eh?

Red Cross last night and volunteer [for] tea fest. Emily and I went to C-Shop in the evening. It's not the way it used to be.

P.S. Again. The army's taken over the two top floors of Eckhart [Hall]. Do you think they'll blow up my Phy Sci class?

Monday, February 2, 1942

Hello. Life goes on. Today was the funniest day. Dark close sky that looked as though you could touch it with your fingertips and red west from four o'clock on. I walked out of Billings feeling sort of light. The way you must feel when you're drunk or something. My limbs were somewhere far beneath me and the world seemed to be contracting and dilating about me

---

*The line is actually "Stick close to your desk." It comes from Sir Joseph Porter's song "When I Was a Lad" in the William S. Gilbert and Arthur Sullivan operetta *H.M.S. Pinafore; or, The Lass That Loved a Sailor*.

as though size were an uncertain figure and was constantly changed. Everything swam before me as in a mirage. Even underneath the solid earth was changed. It was as if I were walking upon sponges. Uncertain of anything. I felt so woozy I went into Cobb to recuperate. I studied for a while. Even there the chair I sat on seemed unsteady and it was as if the earth were breathing underneath me. Verra peculiar day. . . .

I get bored dreadfully with everything. I don't know what's wrong with me. I think I'm the intellectual type and should spend more time on my studies.

Wednesday, February 4, 1942

Hello. Awful wet snow out today and everyone skidding around and laughing and sniffling. Went to Phy Sci at nine o'clock and it was wonderful. Galaxies and galaxies of stars and all circling round and our sun, some much larger than we, only a tiny bare light in the firmament. Phy Sci is a real subject. I'm getting so I like it. It gives you something. Studied three hours this afternoon—part in Cobb Hall, part in Oriental Institute with the mummies—one kind or another. Donald Weeks from my French class asked me out for Saturday but I told him I couldn't. He's a nice boy though.

Had a very peculiar dream last night and woke up still dreaming it. I will relate it here as I have nowhere else to tell it.

Well, to begin with, the situation was this: we were in a house surrounded by a small garden or yard. We were a nondescript group of about 20 people, myself in there and Miriam Petty that I remember and one young man I do not know. But as to the rest whether they were friends or strangers, I cannot say. Anyhow, we were in this house—or outside of it and all about us were flames—at first far away and then later getting closer and closer.

Somehow everyone there knew that the whole earth ("world" I said in my dream) was aflame, through some catastrophe or what I do not know, and knew also that we were the last people alive and that soon we too would perish in the flames. But outwardly it didn't seem to affect us. . . . We were as calm or rather they were as calm as if life stretched ahead of them forever. That was what astonished me. "Don't they realize," I thought, "that in a few hours we will be consumed?" But when I mentioned it, it was as if I had said an awful thing to speak openly of our impending doom. "Let us at least," said a voice, "die like ladies and gentlemen, like human beings." "But there will be no one even to know we did," I protested.

"Let there be no hysteria among us," was repeated.

So I was silenced and only once remarked that I wondered if I should smell like roast beef. And even the humor of that seemed unappreciated.

They were all calm, as though really it didn't affect them and I began to think perhaps it didn't. Some of them were playing bridge outside.

Meanwhile the flames kept getting closer and closer and as if I were far away I would see our small island of shelter surrounded by fire.

The young man and I explored the limits of our rapidly shrinking safety zone and seemed, I cannot remember it clearly, very excited as the flames licked closer and on the verge of doing something—I do not know what, but it apparently was of great moment.

The other people continued to move about as phlegmatic as before.

At this point I can remember no more. My last sensation is that of thinking: in a few moments I shall be burning—will it hurt? Will it last long? And then thinking again: No one will ever know; we are the last people that are.

That is all I remember, but I was not alone at the end. Perhaps we still anticipated some action. There seemed to be a hurry about us.

Isn't that a peculiar dream? I suppose I can trace most of the symbols in it. So often have I seen cartoons in the paper of the earth aflame and our America the last stronghold. Now lately we realize that even this too is catching fire and that we also shall perish. . . . As to the indifference of the people. That is what astonishes me truly about the war in the people around me. Somehow they have kept aloof from it. As I say, no one seems affected. The day war was declared, we played bridge with impassive faces after hearing the declaration.

At least I hope we can do as the voice in my dream said: die like ladies and gentlemen, like human beings, without hysteria. . . .

Well, now, time to go to sleep. I baked a chocolate chip cake last evening. My first and delicious! I'm going to eat a piece now and go to sleep. That was a dream, wasn't it?

Night!

Tuesday, February 10, 1942

Hello. Singapore a-falling! All the faery-tale capitals of the world. This started a long time ago with Addis Ababa.

School today. The clocks have been set back one hour or rather ahead, I guess—anyhow we get up an hour earlier—so I slept through MVC this morning. They call it Wartime, not Daylight, Savings. After school, Betty and I went to C-Shop. Then as it was snowing, we went out to play in the snow. Lots of Coast Guards around. They live in Burton [dormitory] now, you know, and drill all over Midway. Solemnly watched us build—or try to—a snowman. But the snow wouldn't pack. . . .

Had fight with Mom. Quite jolly.

Daddy's still working nights. It's awful hard on him.

Dreamt last night I was soldier in Philippines. The Japs snuck into our fort and I lassoed them all with measuring tape and captured them. Didn't feel at all human in my dream. No thinking: after all, they are human beings. All I thought was to get rid of them. My baser side in dreams, I guess.

*Thursday, February 12, 1942**

School even today. Lincoln's birthday, of course, but it's not supposed to be patriotic to have holidays now. Wartime, you know. Tomorrow Mr. Ashford is going to set off an incendiary bomb in Phy Sci. If I don't reappear, you'll know why.

Worked in *Maroon* office this morning. Practiced my French poem, "La feuille"—by [Antoine Vincent] Arnault. Recited to Mr. Bond. He said I was purty good—even asked me if I had had French before. Then to C-Shop. . . . Bridge.

Donald Weeks came over and asked me for a toboggan outing with Snell Hall a week from Sunday—I said OK—he's a nice boy.[†]

---

*This entry is the last one from the existing diaries.

†At the toboggan outing, Joan met Bob Morrison, a graduate student in chemistry at the University of Chicago—and her future husband.

...ever get there. Tuesday Bet
ednesday, Purr, Thursday
a Tabbe. I swore no one
...up to stop me today. Test
...Erica came along & we both
...sat out law fling. I saw
...rica. But she departed
...& over there without her & t
...st as I was slipping into
...hy sci- I heard her litt
...ee "Joan". But I was determin
...ed Dragged her back with
...e... and her friend too
...One girl who had a comp
...at already. Then Bill ca
...and sat down next to
...e. Stevenson was very go
...day — Funny and all
...e poured carbon dioxi-
...you couldn't see it) into
...a paper bag & it went d
...was spooky. Other ex
...th gasses too. (He's so
...lish. Yesterday he left

1943

 # Age 20

"Truth does not burn."

Spring 1943
*"Morale in Wartime: With Special Emphasis on Morale Factors and Problems in World War II"**

Victory in the present war has been said to depend upon which of the warring countries can maintain the highest morale. Certainly in this war, more than ever before, especially civilian morale takes on a new importance. Much has been written and said, especially in Germany, about the fact that the defeat in 1918 was due not to the physical defeat of the German armies but to a collapse of the "Home front," i.e., of civilian morale. Certainly this is at least true in part. . . .

---

*This entry came from Joan's school notebook; these notes are for a paper with this title.

No country can go on fighting when its citizens fail to perceive an object for their sacrifices. In this country we have heard, again and again, on the radio and in the newspapers, of the "coming breakdown of German morale." We are told that the German people could not sustain a defeat like that of the British at Dunkirk and that their morale is maintained only while one victory follows another. It is true that the German morale has not been exposed to any "trial by fire" such as the British experienced in the summer of 1940. But it is also true that the Germans have been subjected to a well-formulated and deliberate plan to increase their morale. Only recently have American and British sociologists and psychologists been employed by the government to study civilian morale and to advise methods of improving it. The German government has followed such a policy since 1935.

Every war is a "holy war."

Army morale presents special problems. Authorities are agreed that it is not on the front that morale problems arise but in the "between times," the periods of "Sitzkrieg,"* that morale begins to falter. Every effort must be made at this time to help the soldier normally busy and occupied. Letters from home should not be lists of grievances, the German High Command announces in its "Handbook for Women," but it would not hurt if they contained references to bombing raids of the enemy. These will serve to rouse the soldiers' anger.

---

*"Sitting war." This is a play on the term *Blitzkrieg* (German for "lightning war"), which was sometimes called the Phoney War. It occurred between the invasion of Poland in 1939 and the invasion of France, Norway, and the Low Countries in the spring of 1940.

"Desertion" or "defeat" are two words conspicuously missing from the German "Handbook of War"; it is never acknowledged that anything but victory is possible. . . .

Special Problems in World War II

. . . Except in Germany, it is perfectly true our leaders have ignored the psychological effects of conscription and later of war upon a generation which grew up in the intervening 20 year period of World Wars I and II. This generation had grown up exposed to a variety of factual and propagandistic analyses of the first world war. They had come to believe that war was a "racket" created by munitions makers and international bankers and the best recourse was to keep clear of it. Suddenly to throw these children of the "Lost Generation" who grew up with the only too evident reminders that the first world war had accomplished nothing—to throw them into a war with practically the same goals, slogans, and parties was ignoring their very probable negative reactions.

Many times has it been said that the price we paid in ships and airplanes was well worth the unifying result of American indignation over Pearl Harbor. Many people are fighting in a war which they cannot fully believe in—they are defending something rather than fighting for it. That is why it is important while we are still fighting war to formulate our peace objectives and give meaning to what seems to many to be only another futile struggle. . . .

Good morale requires not only desire for victory, and belief that victory will be good, but also faith that victory will ultimately be achieved. . . . Archibald MacLeish* remarks

---

*An American poet.

that even Hitler's ruffians recognize the power of books to be great—they acknowledge this by burning them.

But truth does not burn and lies become no more real.

Tuesday, February 2, 1943*

I remember the clear cold day we met
All ice and shining snow and sun dazzling but chill.
The trees black and lacy against the snow-hills
And the figures of people standing out clear on the
    landscape.
You, with your green changing eyes turning to look at
    me
As I stood on the hill. . . .

War, even the war is beautiful, because it is so
    expected.
This world could not exist if there were not the under-
    tone of tragedy.
The black shape is always moving
Across the face of the bright moon.

The songs that are trite to us now
May make us weep sometime because they bring back
Days that were when everything was yet to be done
And the world lay far below us—
Still to be ventured.
"I don't want to walk without you, baby" . . .
"I left my heart at a stage-door canteen" . . .
"This is worth fighting for. . . ."†
We may even cry because we remember

---

*From Joan's poetry notebook.
†These are all lines from popular songs of the time.

That "Mr. Five by Five"* made us smile once
And the "Strip Polka"† will seem quaint and
   old-fashioned.

Maybe we'll remember then
The day we first met
On a hill, while the world lay below us
Painted with black trees on snow
Traced with the steaming breath of cows
And black wisps of smoke from chimneys
And hills beyond and a white road—
And the world—
Still to be ventured.

Darling, if we come to nothing
Let's not forget that.
Let's not forget
We stood on top of the world once.‡

---

*A song from 1942 about a man "five feet tall and five feet wide." Harry James and others made it popular.
†A song by Johnny Mercer, including the immortal lines often intoned by my father: "'Take it off, take it off,' cries a voice from the rear." The song was made popular by the Andrews Sisters in 1942.
‡Joan married Bob on June 19, 1943.

Acknowledgments

This book could not have come to light without the help and encouragement of many people. First of all, thanks to my brothers, Bobby and Jimmy, and their families, for supporting and encouraging this tribute to Joan. I know they'll recognize the mother they knew and loved in this teenage girl. To my cousin, Jeanne Hawkins, for supporting me as I went through family documents at a hard time. And to Beverly Smith, who tirelessly transcribed Joan's poetry and gave my father, Bob, a cheerful presence after Joan's death. To Nicky Nicolasa, for all her love for my parents in their final years, enabling them to live at home together. And to many neighbors for nurturing and nourishing Joan.

I consulted with numerous writers when I had questions or queries. I am grateful to Joan's longtime friends and fellow "Scribblers" members, Marge Keyishian and Carole Rogers, for giving me honorary membership into their writing circle. Also Laura Cottam Sajbel, for encouraging me in Austin. In England, two friends were convinced of this project's merits and helped support me as I worked on it: Pamela Neville-Sington and Carey Robinson.

Bunni and Frank Lambert offered me a lifeline to the University of Chicago in the late 1930s and early 1940s, as well as a new friendship in the 21st century. Don Ritchie, John Ware, George Hunt, Susan Ferber, Jeff Kleinman, Lorraine Ash, and Tina Kelley all were perceptive and thoughtful in their responses to my queries. And various colleagues gave me good advice; to them, I offer thanks. They include Claudia Nelson, Elizabeth Makowski, Mary Brennan, Caroline Jones, Marilynn Olson, and Teya Rosenberg. At U-High, various people kindly offered information and a vital photo: Kay Kirkpatrick, Chris Janus, Kerry Tulson, David W. Magill, Susan Shapiro, and Earl Bell. The education you offer at your wonderful institution sustained Joan for many decades.

Lisa Reardon was an exceptional editor; she seemed to be channeling how I wanted the volume to look. Her vision enabled the production of Joan's memoir. To her, I am eternally grateful. And kudos to Kelly Wilson, copyeditor extraordinaire.

My husband, Jim Kilfoyle, and children, Sarah and John, lived with this project for almost two years and always showed compassion and good humor. Jim picked up the pieces of my shattered heart after my parents' deaths. Sarah, an ever-perceptive teenage girl, jokingly called Joan "Emo-Grandma"—one emotive teenage girl reaching out across the decades to another. I think she will recognize certain family traits in her grandmother as a teenager. And John, whose tender heart always moved him to give me a spontaneous hug when I was sad, giggled at humorous tidbits I shared during the editing process. I hope you kids will enjoy the humanity in the mythic presence of your grandmother.

And, finally, to my parents, whose love has always encouraged and sustained me. Mom, you spoke of the "Morrison Writing Factory." It still continues, and I'm thrilled we could write a book "together." I just wish you were with me to see it published. To both of you, love always.

Index

245

INDEX

INDEX

Wehlen, Joan
 appearance, 5, 23, 29, 51, 92, 102,
  123, 148, 154, 166, 172, 176–77,
  178, 192, 197
 birthdays, 21, 87, 153, 220–21
 blessing the world, 113–14
 career goals, 14, 15, 55, 101
 clothes, 29, 37, 49, 61, 67–68, 70,
  88, 102, 109–10, 117, 126, 130,
  156, 188, 194, 197, 201
 confirmation, 16–17, 25
 family residences, 19, 83, 141–42,
  158–59
 grades, good, 31, 55–56, 111, 196,
  204, 208, 211, 220, 226–27
 grades, poor, 44, 171, 181, 210
 grandmother, 198, 216
 health, 156, 160, 164, 172, 174–75,
  179, 182, 221. See also tubercu-
  losis tests
 intelligence, 31, 44, 55, 148, 218,
  219, 232
 personality, 32, 148, 172, 219
 popularity, 50–51, 92, 148, 155
 school memories, 32–33, 191–93
 study habits, 17, 124, 172, 183, 209,
  220, 227, 232
 tardiness, 29, 32, 36–37, 70
 teeth, 81, 142, 206, 230
 weight, 23, 83, 92, 146, 172
 work at factory, 194–97, 198
 writing ability, 14, 15, 17, 54, 55,
  58, 79, 208
Wehlen, Mr. Werner (Joan's father)
 appearance, 177–78
 birthday, 67
 gifts, 124–25
 going to movies, 204, 206, 208
 with Joan, 10–11, 42, 51, 158, 181,
  219, 220, 222–23
 Joan's factory job, 194–95
 at lake, 59
 listening to radio, 177, 185
 playing with Joan, 81–82, 101
 progressive education and, 104, 122
 relationship with Joan, 88, 177–78,
  221
 shopping with Joan, 60
 Swedish family, 198
 Swedish language, 84
 work, 235
Wehlen, Mrs. Neva (Joan's mother)
 going to movies, 58, 124, 161

 with Joan, 5, 14, 22, 35, 42, 49, 72,
  74, 88, 97, 117, 145, 160, 185,
  216
 Joan's mementoes, 82
 playing with Joan, 81–82, 119
 progressive education and, 104, 122
 reading with Joan, 41
 wartime activities, 230
 work, 177, 179, 181, 183, 195
Wehlen, Nils-Erik, 198
Wehlens, marriage, 48, 54, 67, 104,
  156, 159, 164–65, 179
Welles, Orson, 223
Westfal, Doris, 114
What a Life (film), 115
Wheeler, Caroline, 109
White Woman (film), 203
Willis, Father, 108, 122
Willkie, Wendell, 171, 193
Wolf, Arnold, 20, 31
Wolf, Nick, 108
word associations, 21–22
World War II. *See also specific countries
  and leaders*
 beginning of, 134
 casualties, 215
 expansion of war, 173, 176, 178,
  190
 list of events, 176
 morale during, 237–40
 Pearl Harbor bombing, 212–13,
  239
 rumors of attacks in US, 214
 US involvement in, 212–13, 216,
  239
worms, 84
Wright, Rosalind, 109
writing
 journals, 14, 54, 55, 134, 224, 229
 observations about, 40–41
Wyvern Club, 183, 184, 202, 206,
  218, 220, 226

Yerke, René, 209, 211, 215, 219, 226,
  228
Yes, My Darling Daughter (play), 180
Young, Father, 53–54
Yugoslavia, 178, 181

zeppelins, 5–6, 24
Zog, King, 116
Zola, Émile, 221